Who is GOD
for the
First Nations People

by

Sarah Tun

(c) 2017

Who is God for the
First Nations People

Larus Press

ISBN: 978-0-9949643-2-8

ISBN (eBook): 978-0-9921518-6-7

Cataloguing data available from Library and Archives Canada

To order: http://www.sarahtunwordsandvoices.com

or

http://www.laruspress.com

Available on Amazon and other leading sites

LarusPress is a publishing imprint of books written and produced by Sarah Tun

To contact: Email: info@LarusPress.com

www.LarusPress.com

Dedication

This book is dedicated to the people of Constance Lake First Nations Reserve near Hearst, Northern Ontario. I respect and admire you for your integrity and courage, and thank you for opening your lives and your culture to me.

Acknowledgements

I'd like to thank Father God and Yeshua, also known as the Lord Jesus, for saving me from a life of misery. I'd like to thank the Holy Spirit for being with me, showing me my strengths and my weaknesses, so that I could be an overcomer and live an abundant life. I'd like to thank my family for their love and support, and my spiritual families from churches and fellowships I've been involved with around the globe, but in particular to Bethel Church, Kingston, Ontario, the Pentecostal Church in Constance Lake First Nations, and Daystar. Each of these groups enabled me to build wonderful relationships amongst those at Constance Lake.

May my words inspire as God would intend. May all who love the Lord be encouraged and blessed. May those who come to discover him through these pages be forever changed into the likeness of Yeshua.

Why read this Now?

I believe every day matters and that this book will change your life if you take what I'm saying at my word and allow Yeshua into your heart.

Time is short! The evil in the world is on the rise and I believe our days, as we experience life on this planet now, are coming to an end soon. I believe God is going to intervene in a new and supernatural way and we need to be ready. You can read various things I've posted in my blog about that at http://www.LarusPress.com

I don't believe there is time to waste. We need to be sure we're right with God for our own betterment and for His delight.

As you open the pages of this book it is my prayer that you will discover new truths about the Creator God whom you know, that will allow you to experience more hope, more joy, more love and more inspiration than ever before.

Shalom - God's Peace - and Blessing.

Sarah Tun

Table of Contents

Prologue

God gave me a word for the First Nations people while I was at an intercessors meeting in 2015, praying for our nation of Canada: The word was,

"God is delighted with the First Nations because they preserve life."

First Nations people do not practise abortion.

I have friends at Constance Lake First Nations, Northern Ontario. I first went to Constance Lake with my church, Bethel in Kingston. I went there to teach the children about Jesus, and later to meet women, to build relationships and long term bonds. It is through these relationships that this booklet was born.

I have a picture in my mind of a warrior in profile. He's leaning against a wall, his shoulders are slightly bent. He wears ancient style clothing suitable for summer, with no headdress but just a feather, slightly droopy, is on his head. He is looking nowhere in particular. Is he dejected? Is he waiting? Has he lost a battle? I don't know, but I see that he is proud yet humble. He is alone.

It is my prayer that the words in this book will speak the universal languages of Truth, Love, Forgiveness and Grace to a culture of people with Dignity, Generosity, Humour and Brokenness, people who deserve to know the freedom of salvation and the life-giving message of the Creator's will: to have the Kingdom on Earth as it is in Heaven.

A word about the name of the Son of God: Yeshua is his Hebrew name, the name he was given at birth. However, in most translations of the Bible the translators use the Greek translation of his name, which is Jesus. Such is the Bible translation I have used most, which is the New King James Version (NKJV). There are Bibles which use the original Hebrew name for the Saviour, such as Tree of Life version (TLV); Jewish scholars who believe in Yeshua have published this translation. I have mostly used NKJV but where indicated, I have used TLV to emphasise the Hebrew roots of the Son of God.

May 2017

PART 1:
THE STORY

CHAPTER 1

From the Beginning to Today

It is my understanding that the First Nations people are a people of stories. I am not a great storyteller, but the Creator God is. We don't know when His story began but before time He created a universe, and then He created mankind so that He would enter into relationship with people. He made people unique from all other living creatures. Man had not only a body and a soul, but also a spirit. Through rebellion against God, Man's spirit died. But God made one way so that his spirit could be revived. Then God could be in fellowship with him again.

I understand that First Nations people, by tradition, believe other living creatures have a spirit. There are other spirits, but I'm here to say that there is one particular spirit which comes from God while others do not. This difference will unfold through the pages. For now, let us begin with the beginning of the Universe, time and mankind.

To know God the Creator, we start before the beginning of time.

"In the beginning God created the heavens and the earth. The earth was without form, and void; and

darkness *was* on the face of the deep. And the Spirit of God was hovering over the face of the waters." (Genesis 1:1-2)

There is one Creator of the whole Universe; he is God. There is the Spirit of God who existed before time. And there is one story in human history that reveals Creator God to us.

The story begins with Creation. But how do we know the story is true, when there are no people to testify to what occurred before the beginning of time?

Reader, you will appreciate the value of oral stories. But the stories that tell us who the Creator is began over six thousand years ago, even before people were on the earth.

God ensured the stories would be kept. He appointed a chosen group of people to write them down and preserve them. As I share with you who these chosen people are, you'll discover they are not so very different from you. And through God's relationship with them, you will discover who this God is, and how He is your God too.

God's Chosen People

The story of the Hebrew people began four thousand years ago.

While the Creator of the Universe has made Himself available to all, He is not white, He is not European. His chosen people are Jewish, originally from Hebrew tribes in the Middle East. He chose them because of one man's faith toward God. The man's name was Abram, whom God renamed Abraham ("father of many").

From Abraham was born a specific people group called the Hebrews who were brown in skin colour and began as a tribal nation of twelve tribes. They were Creator God's chosen people; it is to them He gave His laws and blessings, which revealed to them who He is. He gave the law and the prophets to these people and told them to write down the laws and history of these people. He was in fellowship with them. He fulfilled a promise which He made to their forefather Abraham, a promise of land. He told Abraham he would be the father of a great nation. That nation was to become the mighty nation of Ancient Israel.

The story these Hebrew people wrote down and saved became a series of scrolls they called the Tanakh. Today, this record is known in the world as the Old Testament of the Bible.

Why did God choose this particular group of people to preserve His story? And why was it necessary to keep this story?

Fellowship between God and Mankind

The Creator God has always wanted fellowship with mankind. According to the Tanakh He made man in His image and to have relationship with him. We see God in all of His creation, but to have personal relationship with Him is His desire for us. And so, He made a man, breathed His own spirit into the man to give him life, and made him unique from all the other creatures that He made.

The creation of mankind is where the story begins.

Adam and the beginning of humankind

After the beginning of time, God created the first man, Adam and they walked in fellowship together. This was about six thousand years ago. But God did not want man to be alone as the only human being, and so He made woman too, and Adam called her Eve. They lived in peace with God.

But one day Adam rebelled and broke the only commandment God had given him. He and Eve were sent out from God's presence. From that time onward, mankind grew more and more rebellious.

Over 1500 years passed. The earth became populated, concentrated in what we now call the Middle East. But most of mankind was evil. Every person born had inherited the rebellion of Adam, and the world was not serene and peaceful as God had intended, but was full of violence, decadence, greed and cruelty.

During the 1500 years that passed, God observed the evil of man on the earth. He wiped out most of mankind in a flood to start civilisation again. Still there was much evil. So next God separated people by causing them to speak different languages so they couldn't communicate together. Mankind then began to migrate across the globe, and perhaps this is when the First Nations people left the Middle East and moved across the north eventually to arrive in the Americas.

Still there was evil in the world and mankind did not worship their Creator.

Abraham

But God found a man who unlike most, had faith in his Creator. To this man God gave an instruction and made a promise. God named this man Abraham and promised him that God would make him the father of a great nation. God said He would bless this man, make his name great, and that he would be a blessing.

God had waited for this man with whom He could have fellowship, and from whom He would create a great nation that would demonstrate to the rest of the world the glory, majesty and goodness of the Creator. A nation that would worship the Creator God and uphold His ways would be a model for all mankind. Through this nation, people would see how God had always intended mankind to live.

He instructed Abraham to leave his home and God would lead him. Abraham took the instruction and left his home in Ur (now a part of Iraq) and migrated to Canaan (part of which is now the country of Israel).

At this point, Abraham was just a man with a promise from God. But God was faithful. Abraham had sons and through one of them, the land of Canaan did eventually become the great country God had promised to Abraham.

God had waited for the father from whom His chosen people would descend. Generations of God's chosen people were born. They developed into a tribal nation called the Hebrews, left the land of Canaan and became honoured guests in the land of Egypt. But eventually they became their slaves. They held onto their stories and their faith in a Creator God and a Promised Land, but they would have to re-enter that Promised Land before the nation of Israel could be formed.

It was hundreds of years before it would grow to be the nation most envied in the world.

Moses and the Promised Land

Four thousand years since Abraham walked the earth we can still track the history of the Hebrew people because one descendent of Abraham began to record the history of Creation and of the Hebrew people. That person was Moses.

Five hundred years after the life of Abraham, a Hebrew named Moses was born a slave in Egypt. He would do two significant things that would bring the Hebrews closer to God and to their Promised Land.

First, Moses spoke to God.

Creator God appeared to Moses in a burning bush that did not burn up. He told Moses to go to the Egyptian Pharaoh and demand the Hebrew people be permitted to worship God. Moses asked the Creator His name. God answered, tell them "I AM" has sent you.

Moses debated with God because he didn't really want to go back to Egypt (he had escaped) and face Pharaoh. God was patient and although He would not back down from His instruction to Moses, He communicated with Moses and allowed Moses to argue back. He also promised help for Moses when he returned to Egypt.

Moses did return to Egypt and ensured the Hebrew people came out of slavery, so they would be free to move into their Promised Land. It was Moses who parted the Red Sea, so that the Hebrews could escape from the Egyptians and go into the desert.

The second significant thing that Moses did was to write the history of God's creation and of His chosen people.

Moses had been raised by an Egyptian princess even though he was a Hebrew, so as a child he received an excellent education. He was able to write.

After Moses led the people into the desert he went up a mountain to pray. When he returned down the mountain, he came back with the laws of God on tablets of stone. These were the Ten Commandments we know today, written by the finger of God. Although this is hugely significant, of equal significance is that Moses actually received from God the words that comprise the first five books of the Tanakh (the Old Testament) and transcribed them. These five books are called the Torah and are the books of the Law upon which all other Old Testament writings rest.

The Bible verses quoted at the beginning of this chapter were taken from the first words in the Bible. But if there was no human at the time of creation, how did the words get written into a book form? How did anyone know what to write?

In actual fact, God gave Moses the knowledge and the responsibility to write down the story of Creation on scrolls. Moses also transcribed the events that took place from the beginning of time to the end of his leadership of the Hebrews, as well as God's instructions to the Hebrew people called the Law.

Through the Hebrew people, God gave His instructions to mankind that would ensure health, safety, peace and contentment. The Ten Commandments is only a part of God's Law, which reveals the love and generosity of God, His jealousy, and His faithfulness to honour His promises.

God "dictated" the first five books of what we now call the Bible to Moses. The Hebrew nation called it Torah; to this day the Hebrews (now called Jews) are still called the People of the Book. Part of their purpose has been to preserve the Word of God.

The Hebrews had God's Word. They had the keys to civilisation that the rest of the world lacked; they had the Creator's universal laws and code of conduct that ensured health and blessing. Their nation would prove to be far more civilised than the other nations surrounding them.

Moses died in the desert. Before his death, he looked into the distance to the Promised Land of the Hebrews.

God handed the leadership of the people to a faithful man named Joshua.

The Prophets

God did not abandon the Hebrew people to their own meagre government or laws even after Moses was no longer leading them. When Joshua led them into the Promised Land that would one day be their country, he took with them the scrolls that were the laws and history of God's people.

Before Joshua led the people into their Promised Land, God instructed Joshua and said to be of good courage and, "This Book of the Law shall not depart from your mouth, but you shall meditate in it day and night, that you may observe to do according to all that is written in it. For then you will make your way prosperous, and then you will have good success." (Joshua 1:8)

For another fifteen hundred years there were judges and then prophets, people of God who led the people differently from how other nations were led. Much was recorded on scrolls; so the Tanakh was expanded.

The prophets of God were the Creator's mouthpieces. They heard from God and told the Hebrew people — and sometimes their neighbours — the will of God, His satisfaction or dissatisfaction with them, and the future of the nation.

Eventually the great nation of Israel was formed. It was remarkable, for a time. There were many battles and the

Hebrews defeated their enemies when they obeyed God. However, the people turned from God repeatedly until God allowed the nation to be divided, and then to collapse entirely. Although most of the Hebrew people were dispersed and were sent into exile, the nationality never died out entirely. Today, the small nation of Israel exists and is filled with people of Hebrew descent.

Even after the chosen people had turned their back on God and the nation of Israel had collapsed and most were sent into exile from the land, Creator God still provided prophets to the people. Prophecies were given and were recorded as part of the growing Tanakh that promised a Messiah, a saviour to the Hebrew people, one who would rescue them from their suffering.

Throughout the ancient history of the Jewish people, God ensured the record was kept. The Old Covenant — today usually called the Old Testament by non-Hebraic peoples — includes the books from the beginning of Creation to the end of God's prophets.

Then a time came when God fell silent. For some two hundred years there were no prophets to the people of Israel.

One of the last prophets, the Prophet Malachi, promises in the final chapter of his prophecies, "The Sun of righteousness arise with healing in his wings; and ye shall go forth, and grow as calves of the stall." (Malachi 4:2)

Names of Creator God

God chose a nation to keep His Word for future generations, and He related to the prophets who wrote the scrolls as guided by the Holy Spirit. He related to these people and they had many names for this God, who was close to them and not distant. Some of His names (in Hebrew) are:

Yehova (I AM, The One Who is the Self-Existent One)

Abba (Daddy, Father)

Adonai (The Lord)

Elohim (The All-Powerful One, Creator)

El Roi (The God Who Sees Me)

El Shaddai (The All Sufficient One, The God of the Mountains, God Almighty)

Emmanuel (God With Us)

Yehova-Rapha (The Lord Who Heals)

Yehova-Rohi (The Lord is My Shepherd)

Yehova-Tsidkenu (The Lord Our Righteousness)

Yehova-Jirah (The Lord Who Provides)

The accuracy of the Tanakh

The details of Hebrew history as revealed in the Tanakh have been confirmed by non-Christian historical documents written throughout history, and further proven from archeological discoveries over decades even up to today. There is no doubt about the accuracy of this ancient history.

Although long dead, Abraham had fathered the nation of Israel; furthermore, he would also father many other nations through his descendant Yeshua, who would impact the world more than any other person in history.

Even before the nation of Israel was born, events had lined up so that the promise the Creator had made to Abraham would be fulfilled. As history continued to unfold, Abraham would become the father of not only the nation of Israel but of many nations, through Yeshua.

Yeshua

Two thousand years after Abraham, and two thousand years before our time, out of the ancient Middle Eastern tribal nation of Israel, a baby was born and was given the name named Yeshua. He came from the tribe of Judah (where the word Jew comes from), which was one of the original twelve tribes of the Hebrews.

Many Biblical prophecies foretold the coming of a Messiah, and the details of Yeshua's birth, life, death and resurrection match every one of these prophecies.

You have probably heard of Yeshua by his translated name, Jesus. He was a Jewish Rabbi (teacher) in Israel who lived, taught, died and was resurrected; and he changed the world.

Born into a brutal world

Two thousand years ago, the world was brutal. The Laws of Israel were not practiced worldwide and the God of the Hebrews was largely unknown. God had given a code that would allow people to live in peace, health and prosperity but it was not practised except by a remnant of Hebrew descendants. There was little consciousness of goodness, kindness or forgiveness in the world.

Into that violent and rebellious world, the Creator God sent His son, who was born to a Hebrew virgin. He arrived in the broken nation of Israel, the nation Creator God had begun long before with Abraham. Once it had been a great nation of influence, wisdom and wealth. But it had not been faithful to God and so had been invaded over the centuries. It had eventually shrunk in power and size.

At the time of Yeshua's arrival, Israel was a nation that was sidelined and oppressed, ruled by a Roman government who allowed the Jews their cultural and religious practices but did not respect their Hebrew identity and did not engage with them.

The virgin who mothered the baby was named Miriam — Mary is the non-Hebrew name we are familiar with in North America. Yosef — or in English Joseph — became her husband and the adoptive father to Yeshua. He was told by God to name the baby Yeshua (which means "to deliver") and it was not until that moment in time that the Hebrew Messiah had a name.

Yeshua grew up and learned his adopted father's trade, that of carpentry. But when he was thirty, he began his ministry to the chosen people, the Jews.

First he was baptised; he was immersed in water to demonstrate any who seek to follow him must be cleansed from their old life of sin and profess their faith in and desire to follow God's ways. Then he was tempted by the devil and overcame that temptation. Finally, he moved around

Israel, healing the sick, cleansing people from evil spirits and raising some from the dead.

He taught, speaking to crowds of people who marvelled at his works of healing and his words of wisdom. He taught the people to look at the world in an entirely different way, not to see what they could gain but rather, what they could give. He modelled the image of God as forgiving and blessing His people, and encouraged them to turn back to God and rebel no more. In so doing, he shifted the way people thought and related to one another as well as to God.

He had faithful disciples who ministered with him and many stuck by him until he was arrested.

The Chosen People Rejected their Messiah

There are hundreds of ways that the person Yeshua fulfils the Hebrew promise of their Messiah. He came specifically for the Jewish people. But just as prophecies foretold his coming, so too did prophecies foretell that his own people would reject him, just as they rejected his father, the Creator of the Universe.

One day during his ministry, Yeshua went into a synagogue, a holy house of the Jewish faith. He was passed one of the scrolls and began to read as was the custom. He read, "The Spirit of the Lord is upon me, because he has anointed me to preach the gospel to the poor; he has sent me to heal the brokenhearted, to proclaim liberty to the captives and recovery of sight to the blind, to set at liberty those who are oppressed; to proclaim the acceptable year of the Lord." (Luke 4:18-19) The people were staring at him and then he said, "Today is this scripture fulfilled in your hearing." (Luke 4:21) The people were astonished and mumbled about him. He said, "Assuredly I say to you, no prophet is accepted in his own country." (Luke 4:24)

Yeshua was not surprised that the people would reject his ministry.

The many miracles that Yeshua performed brought him much popularity. The message of forgiveness was welcomed by those who were poor, by outsiders, sinners, or people of bad character.

The leaders of the Hebrew traditions were jealous and fearful of this popular rabbi who contradicted their laws (which were actually add-ons and interpretations of God's Laws that were not from God). They sought to have Yeshua charged and crucified. They stirred up many against him. Ultimately, many of the chosen people of God rejected their long-awaited Messiah and brought a curse upon themselves that would bring to the nation agony and death over the centuries.

Death and Resurrection of Yeshua

Yeshua was falsely accused of blasphemy (speaking offensively about God), arrested, tried and crucified. He died on a cross, the usual Roman way of executing people at the time.

Three days later, as prophecies predicted, he was raised from the dead.

There is no question that he died or that he was raised from the dead. There are many witnesses to both facts, even though the Jewish leaders tried to hide the facts.

Yeshua taught many valuable lessons and performed many miracles. But it is through his resurrection that those who believed, then and throughout the ages even until now, are resurrected into new life spiritually. Yeshua appeared to many people after his resurrection as proof it happened. When he eventually returned to the Father in Heaven, he sent his Holy Spirit to us; through that Spirit our spirit is brought to life.

Before Jesus left the earth to be with his Father the Creator, he instructed the faithful disciples to reach out to all people, not only the Jews.

Yeshua is not only for Jewish people

There is a scripture in one of the prophets' writings that says Yeshua came not only for the Jewish people,

"Indeed He says, 'It is too small a thing that you should be my servant to raise up the tribes of Jacob, and to restore the preserved ones of Israel; I will also give you as a light to the Gentiles, that you should be my salvation to the ends of the earth.'" (Isaiah 49:6)

Gentiles are those people who are not Jewish. They are not descended from Abraham, Isaac and Jacob, and are non-Hebrews.

Although his ministry on earth was focused towards the chosen people of Israel, after his resurrection he commissioned his followers to share the story of salvation from sin "to the ends of the earth."

The coming of the Holy Spirit

When Yeshua was teaching his disciples, he foretold his death and resurrection. He also said he would leave them but would send a comforter that would be with them forever. This comforter was the Holy Spirit, the same Spirit who hovered over the earth at creation.

Fifty days after Yeshua's crucifixion, the Holy Spirit came to those who believed in Yeshua as the Messiah of Israel and the Saviour of the world. Tongues of fire were seen above the heads of disciples who were waiting and worshipping Creator God; people started speaking in foreign languages accurately without knowing those languages personally. These were signs of the Holy Spirit.

The Holy Spirit equipped followers with the power and presence of the Creator God. It was time for the people of God to begin to minister to the ends of the earth.

Early Christianity

While the faith leaders of the Jewish people had rejected Yeshua, his disciples had not. After Yeshua's death and resurrection, the Jewish group of believers became known as Christians and Christianity was born. The earliest Christians were Jewish, who then took the truth of Yeshua to non-Jewish people as well.

Christianity developed after Yeshua's life on earth and was shared throughout the Middle East, then carried into Rome and Spain. It was named Christianity, which came from the Greek word 'Christ' which means 'Saviour'. The early followers made up the church (the word church referred to people who believed, not a building), who sought to live as Yeshua had taught. Loving God, loving your neighbour as yourself and doing good to your enemies was the lifestyle that Yeshua introduced into an otherwise barbaric world. The preaching and teaching of Yeshua's followers spoke about God's love for mankind, of salvation, and of the eternal life that faith in Yeshua offered. Some of the earliest leaders wrote of their experience with Yeshua.

From the time he was on earth until today, Yeshua calls each of us to return to relationship with Creator God through faith in him. A part of Christian responsibility includes honouring God and his creation.

Compiling the Bible

The Bible as we know it has two parts, the Old and the New Testaments. It was compiled by the early believers over a period of two hundred years. There were many scrolls that were passed around by the early believers, but some were eventually not considered legitimate parts of God's story; they were not included in the Bible.

After years of consideration and prayer, a total of 66 books became the official Bible that we have today. The Hebrew portion made up of 39 books became what is now known as the Old Testament, and 27 scrolls that were written after Yeshua's ministry made up the New Testament.

There were no printing presses for 1400 years after Yeshua, so copies of the Bible were painstakingly transcribed by hand. Over the centuries, copies of some original scrolls have been discovered which match our existing version, as another testament to the legitimacy of God's Holy word.

Organised Christianity erases the Jewish roots

However, a few hundred years after Yeshua walked on the earth as a man, people got in the way of the pure message from God. Rules were included that weren't part of Yeshua's teaching. Jewish roots were erased because of anti-Semitism (racism against Jewish people) amongst believers.

The white Europeans began to control the church. One of the first things they did was to wipe out the Hebrew/Jewish connections to Yeshua. He would be called by his name in translation, Jesus. He was Jewish, and most of his original followers were Jewish. But the organised church would not call him by his Hebrew name, and the festivals and dates that God gave to His people were officially revised by the established church. The Hebrew festival of Passover, which marked the crucifixion and resurrection of Yeshua for example, was replaced by Easter.

The Jewishness of Yeshua practically forgotten

Christianity originally developed as a branch of the Jewish faith. But many traditional Jews did not welcome it. Although Yeshua was Jewish two things conspired to remove the Jewishness from European Christian history, the Jews' rejection of Yeshua as Messiah and anti-Semitism within the body of believers.

Although the earliest followers of Yeshua were Jewish, he also had many Jewish enemies. The Jewish leaders during his time on earth were the teachers of religion and law. They were the people who conspired to have him crucified. They did not want Yeshua's influence or teaching to contaminate their understanding of God or of His Word, the Tenakh.

The Jews who supported the crucifixion had heaped curses upon themselves, demanding the Romans crucify Yeshua. Centuries later, that curse would trigger hatred and punishment. Jews were labeled "Christ Killers" by many Christians. Art portrayed Yeshua, now always called Jesus, as white, and Anti-Semitism (hatred of the Jewish people) developed throughout history.

The Importance of Yeshua's Jewish Roots

We know about the creation of the world through the account of the Torah; we know about the beginning of time and the beginning of man through this book. We know our Father, the Creator of the Universe, based on what is said in the Tenakh. God chose the Hebrew people and gave them the task to write His story and theirs. The writing was inspired by God's Holy Spirit. These men who wrote the book and followed God's laws were almost all of Jewish roots.

Then Creator God sent his son, Yeshua - Jesus, to bring the people into a deeper understanding of Himself. Yeshua knew the Tenakh, and he taught the value of it. He quoted from it and fulfilled the prophecies about the Messiah.

But over time, most Jewish people rejected the idea of Christianity, and the Gentile Christians rejected the Jewish people as well.

The European white man took over the development of Christianity and blotted out the Jewishness of it.

For the First Nation person, just as you come from a tribal nation who loves the Creator, so did Jesus. Just as your people experienced oppression and cruelty, so did his. His roots are not so very different from your own. He understands you and is not separate or exclusive from you.

Church History

There is a whole history lasting hundreds of years that follows after the Christian Bible was put together. For a long time, Yeshua's teaching was buried in man-made religious practice and contradiction. People believed Jesus died for them but they didn't relate to him personally as he had intended, nor to Father God. Then, with the printing press, more and more people had access to the Bible and began to read for themselves to discover God's message.

While even today there is still mystery, we are getting better at understanding God's Word and practicing it faithfully in the way we understand Yeshua intended.

One major understanding in the 1500's that had been buried for centuries comes from a New Testament letter which a Jewish man named Paul wrote.

Ephesians 2:8-9 says, "For by grace you have been saved through faith, and that not of yourselves; it is the gift of God, not of works, lest anyone should boast."

After centuries of blindness, when believers read this they began to realise that God didn't want good works or sacrifice from mankind, but simple faith, just like the faith that Abraham had had thousands of years before. Over the centuries, people had tried all sorts of things to get good with God, such as paying money, saying certain prayers, doing good works or hitting themselves.

It would take even more time for people to realise the same miracles that Yeshua and his disciples performed by the power of the Holy Spirit could be performed by any believer. We're fairly early into the re-discovery and practice of that truth even now.

Explorers and Missionaries to the New World

One of the greatest damages the white European church did to the message of God was to impose their culture to those they tried to teach.

Yeshua had preached, "Go into all the world and preach the gospel to every creature" (Mark 16:15) and as European countries began to explore the New World, they took that teaching with them, many very enthusiastically.

But the people of the new colonies were neither Christian nor European. The great tragedy is that the majority of missionaries mistakenly blended the good news of Jesus' death and resurrection with their white European culture.

Yeshua and the early church spoke of forgiveness, love and acceptance and practised 'the sick being healed, the dead being raised'; yet, in the 17th to 19th centuries, when explorers crossed to America or into Africa, they took with them disease, social and monetary pride, cultural education and geographical boundaries. They mixed all of this with the simple Gospel (Good News) message that all mankind needs the Creator God and access to him is only possible through Jesus Christ. Sadly, although they intended to preach the pure Gospel of Yeshua, they mixed their flawed European culture into the message.

They contaminated the message and alienated many amongst the very people they aimed to attract.

Cultural Confusion

Yeshua was a Jew – a brown man of Middle Eastern culture. But by the 19th and 20th centuries, messengers spoke of Jesus in the context of their own culture. They forced their style of worship or dress upon the people in the cultures they visited, and assumed Yeshua would endorse it. There is no evidence from anything Yeshua ever said or did that he would have.

Yeshua, who now sits in Heaven at the right hand of God the Father (Acts 2:33), comes to all cultures and colours, not to have them adapt to European or "white" culture, but rather so that he can engage with them, as they are uniquely created. He is Yeshua, the one sent from the Creator of the Universe.

You already know the Creator. Now you know his son Yeshua was not white. Perhaps that will be a window into your accepting him as the Messiah that God intends for you.

The Significance of Israel today

Though four thousand years have passed since God led Abraham to the land He promised, the mountains where God led Abraham still exist, as does the land that God promised him. Today we call this land the nation of Israel. Although the size is much smaller than the land promised to Abraham, the nation still exists, after a history that is rich with joy and sorrow, victory and defeat, success and suffering.

The world is watching the small nation of Israel. It is surrounded by enemies and yet is survives bombs, attempts to force it to relinquish some of its land, and rejection from much of the world. But it refuses to be defeated, and God is watching over it with a protecting arm. He is still their God and they are still His chosen people.

The Creator keeps His promises and even now, the tiny nation of Israel thrives, though surrounded by enemies who declare it should not exist. The existence of Israel is a testament to the character of God who keeps His promises and who blesses those who follow Him.

And there is one more promise that Yeshua made to his disciples which is recorded in several places in the Bible. He is going to return. Some say it will be soon. Some say it will be to Israel. I say it would be good to make sure you've embraced his truths before he returns.

The Gospel

The gospel or 'good news' about Yeshua is an essential part of everything that God's Kingdom offers. There is so much for the human race and for each unique society within it to know and to learn from God. This is not the white man's gospel; it isn't any man's gospel. Its root goes all the way back to Abraham, and the promise that he would be the father a great nation. Through Yeshua, he is in fact the father of many nations. All those who embrace Yeshua receive all the blessings of Abraham and his people.

This includes the First Nations people. Just as Abraham was the ancestor of Yeshua, whatever nation embraces Yeshua, becomes a descendant of Abraham, and receives the blessings that Abraham and all of his descendants are promised.*

Through Yeshua, this process begins with the promise of eternal life with God. This is good news to anyone, of any culture, heralded by many but initiated by one man, Yeshua. He came from a culture oppressed by white leadership at that time; he preached the gospel of love and salvation. Yeshua was hated by the religious leaders of his own culture, but loved by the poor, destitute, marginalised, broken-hearted, oppressed, sexual workers, addicts, cheaters, liars, abused people — anyone hungry for Truth, Life, Love, Hope and Joy.

If you fit into any of the above groups, Jesus — Yeshua — came to love you, to honour you, to forgive you, to heal you, and to give you everlasting life with the Father of creation.

This is Yeshua's gospel of salvation – for anyone who wishes to hear it. While it is only a fraction of the demonstration of God's love, it encourages self-respect, courage, unique identity and purpose, within a universal culture of grace and love.

* God's promises to Abraham included: land, descendants, blessing and redemption (forgiveness and reunion) with God. See Genesis, chapter 12, versus 1 – 3 to read about the covenant promise God made with Abraham.

PART II
THE DETAILS

CHAPTER 2

Who is Yeshua (Jesus)?

"In the beginning was the Word, and the Word was with God, and the Word was God. He was in the beginning with God. All things were made through him, and without him nothing was made that was made. In him was life, and the life was the light of men. And the light shines in the darkness, and the darkness did not comprehend it." (John 1:1-5) Then, "And the Word became flesh and dwelt among us, and we beheld His glory, the glory as of the only begotten of the Father, full of grace and truth." (John 1:14)

Inspired by the Holy Spirit as all Biblical scripture is, this was written by Yeshua's closest friend, John, who walked with him during the ministry on earth.

The Word existed at Creation and was a part of it. Then he became flesh, was born and was given the name Yeshua, which in Hebrew means Messiah. This Yeshua was given the power to heal, forgive and make new anyone who believes in him. This man, who is perhaps more familiar by his non-Hebrew name Jesus, was God's son and he came to earth to minister and teach and save people from spiritual death and mortal sin.

The origin and identity of Yeshua

Yeshua's mother was named Mary — called Miriam in Hebrew. She was a virgin and God the Creator was his Father by the Holy Spirit. It is vitally important to history and to the power of Yeshua to acknowledge this fact.

It is very significant that Mary was a virgin and that this baby did not have an earthly father for two reasons. One, that he had God as his father by the Holy Spirit shows God loves people so much that He sent His own son to show us how to live well. Secondly, Yeshua did not inherit the sin that every other person inherited, through their earthly fathers. For this reason, he could be sacrificed on behalf of all humanity, so that God could again be in relationship with people.

Throughout history, mankind has attempted to draw close to God by making sacrifices. But man is so foul, he can't manage to get things right. God finally put an end to sacrifice by giving His son as a sacrifice, shedding his blood for everyone else.

Did you know that it is through the father that we inherit our blood as well as our sinfulness? Since a man did not father Yeshua, but Father-God-the-Creator did, Yeshua did not inherit sinfulness as did the rest of humankind through Adam. And because he did not inherit sin, he could take our place as a sacrifice because of our sins. His pure and untainted blood was shed, therefore he acts as the only sacrifice God requires.

Now we know that human beings inherit their blood (natural realm) and their sinfulness (spiritual realm) from the father, not the mother. This is an important truth.

What Yeshua said about himself

Yeshua claimed to be the Son of God. Countless times he called the Creator of the Universe Father, which infuriated the religious leaders of the time.

"'You are not greater than our father Abraham who died, are You? The prophets also died! Who do you make yourself out to be?' Yeshua answered, 'If I glorify myself, my glory is nothing. It is my Father who gives me glory—the One of whom you say, 'He is our God.' Yet you do not know Him, but I know Him. If I say I do not know Him, I will be a liar like you. Yet I do know Him and keep His Word. Your father Abraham rejoiced to see my day; he saw it and was thrilled.' Then the Judeans said to Him, 'You're not even fifty years old and you've seen Abraham?' Yeshua answered, 'Amen, amen I tell you, before Abraham was, I am!'"(John 8:53-58 TLV)

Then the leaders tried to stone him, because as you might remember from Part I: The Story, I said that God told Moses to tell the people "I AM has sent me" and the religions leaders speaking to Yeshua would definitely have known that.

More I AM

Of himself Yeshua said, I am the bread of life; I am the living bread; I am the door; I am the gate; I am the way, the truth and the life; I am the light of the world; I am from above; I am the good shepherd. He also said no one comes to the father except through me.

He said, "I and my Father are one." (John 10:30)

We can be sure Yeshua actually said these things

The Bible is a document which is reliable, as proven by science and history. Prophecies found within it have come to pass, as supported by other ancient documents and artefacts, and the subsequent events of history.

The Bible claims to be inspired by the Holy Spirit of God, the same Spirit who hovered over the earth when God created it, and the same Spirit by which Yeshua is God's son.

Each of the forty men who contributed to the sixty-six books of the Bible believed Creator God inspired his words.

In the Bible there are many prophesies forecasting the arrival of the Messiah, the Saviour of the World. We see that history proved the prophecies came to pass and those who follow Yeshua recognise that the prophesies about the Messiah were fulfilled when he was born. His earthly name was never given in the prophecies, but the circumstances surrounding his birth, his life, his death, and his supernatural resurrection match those of the prophecies which were given hundreds of years before.

The Bible was transcribed by men who worked carefully, making copies to ensure God's Word was preserved. There are two Covenants, the Old and the New. The Old contains the Hebrew laws and history as revealed by God to Moses (first five books) and also transcribed by other men (later books) too. The New contains the Gospels and letters composed after the time of Yeshua's ministry on earth. To God, the heritage of His chosen people is vital for all mankind.

In modern times many pieces of evidence have been found which further support the accuracy and truth of the Bible, too numerous to list in this short booklet. One specific example is the discovery of the Dead Sea Scrolls in 1947, scrolls of Bible books that confirmed the accuracy of the Bible we had been using for centuries.

Yeshua is generous and loving: Gentiles can be included in God's family

The Hebrew people were God's chosen people, the keeper of God's Word and the beneficiaries to God's promise to Abraham.

But, ultimately, God wants to have fellowship with all people and through Yeshua's sacrifice we all can. He embraces gentiles and if that embrace draws the chosen tribes of Israel to jealousy and brings them back to Him, in God's eyes, that is even better.

It is simply through their faith in 'Jesus Christ' that, throughout the centuries since Yeshua walked the earth, countless people of many, many nations have become 'adopted' descendants of Abraham. That's a great privilege because God blesses His chosen people in amazing ways.

Gentiles didn't necessarily speak Hebrew. The international language was Greek, just as English is now. So, instead of calling this Saviour by his Hebrew name, believers began to call him Jesus.

Jesus, the son of God, came as the perfect, sinless man, like the man that Adam was before he broke God's instruction and sinned. It is Jesus who makes it possible for others to have fellowship with God, the same fellowship that God intended for Adam and for all mankind. Jesus took our sins, paid the debt we inherited from Adam, and gave us back everlasting life through the Holy Spirit, if we will believe and follow him.

The Creator God is our Father. If we allow His son to take our place of punishment for the sinful nature we inherited from Adam, we are free from sin and that is the beginning of new hope and new life.

Yeshua was and is God's son and it's from Creator God that he got his power and authority. He is a key figure for humanity for two main reasons. First, it was he who taught forgiveness and brotherly love, leading the world out of barbarism; and second, he had the power to die as God's sacrifice for everyone else's failure to follow God. Anyone who believes that Yeshua is the Messiah and Saviour can receive blessing and all the benefits of Yeshua's sacrifice to God.

More than a Saviour

Actually, Yeshua is more than a saviour. It is true that he has delivered any who follow him from spiritual death and that they receive everlasting life in Heaven, which is any believer's destiny. But there is more.

While we are on earth, we who follow him also have new life. This means we no longer have anxiety or shame, guilt or fear, when we surrender our lives to follow him. He makes it possible for us to overcome any spiritual force that is not life-giving. We do not have to wait until our earthly life is over to be free from death. He conquered emotional and psychological death as well.

Other names for Yeshua

Throughout the Bible there are other names that are given to Yeshua that further describe his authority, power, character and personality. Some of these names are as follows:

Prince of Peace, King of kings and Lord of lords, Holy One, Head of the Church, Chief Cornerstone, Rock, Word, Son of God, Son of Man, Judge.

I mentioned in Part I: The Story that he promised to return. When he does, he will come to judge the nations. It is my hope that the people of the First Nations will have embraced him by that time.

CHAPTER 3

Why Yeshua had to come

Two thousand years ago people were barbaric – human sacrifices were common, greed, gluttony and lust were rife. Vengeance was normal; life was cruel. People had drifted far from God and what His intention had been for Mankind.

A Jewish man named Yeshua came to teach God's intentions for humanity and to save people from their own sinfulness. He came with a message of how to live so that the world would be a more peaceful place.

He said, 'forgive your enemies', 'love those who hate you', 'blessed are the meek for they shall inherit the earth'. 'Heal the sick, feed the poor, be humble and serve.' Yeshua had to come to give this healthy perspective. Only God's son — who existed from the beginning with God the Father and the Creator — could offer this understanding of how the world was created to exist, and how mankind was intended to relate to God, to one another, to all living creatures, and to the earth itself.

So, Yeshua — also known as Jesus — came to rescue us from a world view of barbarism.

Prophets foretold the coming of Messiah

Throughout Biblical history there were prophetic words given, declaring there would be a Messiah who would come to the suffering, enslaved Jewish nation of Israel. The prophecies had to be fulfilled, or else God's Word would be a lie.

Through Yeshua would come the offer of salvation. This is found in one of the prophetic books in the Bible, written long before he came to earth. Isaiah records,

"Indeed He [God] says, 'It is too small a thing that you should be My Servant To raise up the tribes of Jacob, And to restore the preserved ones of Israel; I will also give you as a light to the Gentiles, that you should be My salvation to the ends of the earth.'" (Isaiah 49:6)

Gentiles are people who are not descended from the Israelite (Jewish) peoples, who are not God's chosen people.

So the promise of a saviour coming was not only for the Jewish people but for all peoples.

Yeshua (Jesus of Nazareth) fulfilled the prophecies of the Messiah specifically and thoroughly. He came when the Jewish people were most oppressed. Below is a chart listing just some of the prophecies that the coming of Messiah fulfilled. While many other prophets of the Old Testament foretold of the coming the Messiah (for Jews) or Saviour (for Gentiles), these are taken from the Book of Isaiah:

THE PROPHECY	THE FULFILLMENT
The Messiah:	**Jesus of Nazareth:**
Will be born of a virgin (Isaiah 7:14)	Was born of a virgin named Mary (Luke 1:26-31)
Will have a Galilean ministry (Isaiah 9:1,2)	Ministry began in Galilee of the Gentiles (Matthew 4:13-16)

Will be an heir to the throne of David (Isaiah 9:7; 11:1, 10)	Was given the throne of his father David (Luke 1:32, 33)
Will have his way prepared (Isaiah 40:3-5)	Was announced by John the Baptist (John 1:19-28)
Will be spat on and struck (Isaiah 50:6)	Was spat on and beaten (Matthew 26:67)
Will be exalted (Isaiah 52:13)	Was highly exalted by God and the People (Philippians 2:9, 10)
Will be disfigured by suffering (Isaiah 52:14; 53:2)	Was scourged by Roman soldiers who then gave him a crown of thorns (Mark 15L15-19)
Will make a blood atonement (Isaiah 53:5)	Shed his blood to atone for our sins (1Peter 1:2)
Will be widely rejected (Isaiah 53:1,3)	Was unaccepted by many (John 12:37, 38)
Will bear our sins and sorrows (Isaiah 53:4, 5)	Died because of our sins (Romans 4:25; 1Peter 2:24, 25)
Will be our substitute (Isaiah 53:6,8)	Died in our place (Romans 5:6, 8; 2 Corinthians 5:21)
Will voluntarily accept our guilt and punishment for sin (Isaiah 53:7,8)	Jesus took on our sins (John 1:29; Romans 6:10; 2 Corinthians 5:21)
Gentiles will seek Him (Isaiah 11:10)	Gentiles came to speak to Jesus (John 12:20,21)

Will be silent before his accusers (Isaiah 53:7)	Was silent before Herod and his court (Luke 23:9)
Will save us who believe in him (Isaiah 53:12)	Provided salvation for all who believe (John 3:16; Acts 16:31)
Will die with transgressors (Isaiah 53:12)	Was numbered with the transgressors (Mark 15:27, 28; Luke 22:37)
Will heal the brokenhearted (Isaiah 61:1,2)	Healed the brokenhearted (Luke 4:18, 19)
God's Spirit will rest on him (Isaiah 11:2)	The Spirit of God descended on Jesus (Matthew 3:16; Mark 1:10; Luke 3:22; 4:1)
Will be buried in a rich man's tomb (Isaiah 53:9	Was buried in the tomb of Joseph, a rich man from Arimathea (Matthew 27:57-60; John 19:38-42)
He will judge the earth with righteousness (Isaiah 11:4,5)	Jesus was given authority to judge (John 5:27; Luke 19:22; 2 Timothy 4:1,8)

(Michal E. Hunt, "Isaiah's Prophecies of the Messiah fulfilled in Jesus of Nazareth" AgapeBibleStudy.com, 2000)

The last of the prophecies listed is to be fulfilled at the second coming, when Yeshua returns to judge the earth.

How the Son of God could make such a difference

Adam, the first man God created, sinned by rebelling against God.

According to Genesis, the first book of the Bible, Adam was formed in God's image. He was the first-born. In fact, male and female were formed in God's image, each being given a body, a soul (mind, will and emotions) and a spirit. It is important to note that for the follower of Yeshua, human-kind is the only living creature who has God's spirit*. While this may be difficult for some First Nations people to recon-cile, those who believe the Bible read that God breathed His spirit into man, but it is not documented that He breathed into any other animal that He created. He made man in His own image, with a living spirit.

But Adam blew it! Eve was deceived into breaking God's command and Adam** disobeyed God knowingly. They both ate fruit from the one tree they were prohibited from eating. Then they tried to hide from the responsibil-ity, adding to their sinfulness.

As a result of this sin, the spirit within them — the spirit God had breathed into them when He created them — died. Their body and soul lived on, but they lost the intimacy with God that they had shared through the Spirit. Next, they were told they must suffer in childbirth and work for their food. Finally, they were exiled from their home, Eden.

Everyone has a biological father. Ever since Adam's sin, every person has inherited that sin through his father. Each of us has been born separated from God, just as Adam had become separated when he ate the one food that had been forbidden.

But Yeshua didn't have an earthly father. So he didn't carry the same sinfulness that all other human beings carry. Only he could restore us back to the Father, not by fathering biologically, but by suffering and dying and taking everyone else's sinfulness onto his sinless self.

Yeshua died for us and sent the Holy Spirit to revive our spirit

Yeshua had to come as a means to reconnect man with God and to give rebirth to man's spirit. The term "born again" refers to new birth and new life, to the rebirth of the spirit within us. Yeshua, as the son of God, restored family back together; he sent the Holy Spirit of God to reignite the human spirit of any person who believes Yeshua is God's son and chooses to follow him.

This unique Holy Spirit offers the following gifts to live within us supernaturally,

"But the fruit of the Spirit is love, joy, peace, long-suffering (patience), kindness, goodness, faithfulness, gentleness, self-control. Against such there is no law." (Galatians 5:22-23)

This Holy Spirit is the only spirit who is Life, Love, and Blessing to mankind. He asks for nothing and requires nothing from us – no gift, no fear, and no appeasement.

Yeshua had to come to restore Israel back to God (Yeshua the Messiah). He also came to save all of us from our rebellion (Jesus the Saviour). Those who have their spirit revived will live with God on the New Earth after their earthly life is ended. But also, while still on earth, those who have their spirit reborn are a new creation, with the opportunity to shed their "Old Man" and step into the "New Man" that God has always intended for them. We are encouraged to, "be transformed by the renewing of your mind." (Romans 12:2) Everything that was before our rebirth is dead. It always was dead actually; we just didn't know it. Now, we can step into new life the moment we surrender our lives to Yeshua and commit to follow him.

Yeshua had to come to save us from our sin and to offer us a means to reconnect with the Creator of the universe in a personal way. His name means 'deliverer'. Even now he delivers anyone who believes in him from the shame, guilt, condemnation, and death which we all share, and offers new life, and a relationship with the Creator God of the universe, if only we believe and follow him.

Because Yeshua was not conceived from a human father, he is the only person who did not inherit sinfulness. Therefore only he can deliver us from our sin.

Yeshua died and rose again, defeating death. Adam was created to live forever but his spirit died when he disobeyed God. Faith in Yeshua revives our spirit.

Eventually, we will even inherit new bodies as well, when Yeshua returns to the earth.

The Role of the Holy Spirit

In the meantime, Yeshua is sitting with God the Father in Heaven. He has sent the Holy Spirit, to comfort and convict us, with his power and presence. That one spirit

– the Holy Spirit –teaches, guides and empowers us, to show us where we are wrong and when we are right. He helps us to love, to forgive, to bless others with God's love, forgiveness and blessing, so that we are free to live in the spirit, as a "New Man." By the power of the Holy Spirit, we are offered life and holiness.

* Living creatures all have a soul, also called a mind, with intelligence, a will and emotions. But only mankind is recorded as having a spirit, that which connects to Father God.

** Note about Eve: Eve is seen in a slightly different light from Adam. Eve was deceived by the serpent, whom the devil inhabited and tempted Eve to eat the fruit which had been forbidden. But Adam was not deceived. He was not tricked as Eve was, but rather deliberately chose to eat what was forbidden. Therefore, while both Adam and Eve ate of the fruit, it is through Adam – and through the male parent ever since – that sin enters man. It is through the Holy Spirit and not a man that Yeshua was conceived, and therefore is born without the sin of Adam. Note about blood: It is also interesting to note that biologically, human beings get all of their blood from their human father. I find it so interesting that thousands of years ago, only God knew that our blood comes only from our fathers. He called for animal blood sacrifice for the Hebrew's sinfulness. But soon after the arrival of Yeshua, no longer were animal sacrifices continued, because the temple where the ceremony was carried out was destroyed. Yeshua had paid the ultimate sacrifice for sin, by bleeding and dying on a cross, and being resurrected again to overcome death and sinfulness. In God's eyes, the Son paid for the sins of mankind, and that ended the need for animal sacrifice.

CHAPTER 4

The Unique Message of Yeshua

At the time Yeshua was born the world was brutal, unforgiving, immoral, and murderous. He preached a way of life that was opposite to the way most people lived. He told stories that taught how to live in love, kindness, mercy, and rightness with God. He offered a message of wisdom and peace. He gave hope, offered absolute forgiveness, and a way to reconnect to the Creator.

But Yeshua was not just a good philosopher or a wise man. The world religions offer many philosophies but not the power of the Creator. However, Yeshua is the son of God; faith in him offers a supernatural rebirth and reunion with Creator God our Father.

Forgiveness comes through God's own sacrifice of His son — and of Yeshua's sacrifice of suffering the pain and death of the cross — not through our own. In no other faith or religion or concept of God is there this promise. At the heart of the full Gospel (which is the good news about being right with God, being free from sin and death, and living in a society that is Heaven on Earth), are three ingredients found nowhere else:

1. Love is the core of our relationship with a sovereign (all knowing, all powerful) Creator God.

2. God sacrificed His own son to pay the penalty for man's sin (which is his separation from God, demonstrated by his unholy actions and thinking). Now we can be in fellowship with God just as He intended us to be from Creation.

3. God is supernatural. His son, Yeshua, was raised from the dead and enables us to overcome our spiritual death by faith (simply by believing and following the Son of God).

Through the supernatural power of God, Jesus overcame death on a cross and was resurrected; this gives him the right to offer eternal life to us too. He now overcomes all pain, anxiety, sickness; when he was on the cross he took all our 'junk' so that we don't have to live with it. The Old Man is dead when we accept Jesus as saviour and Lord. We become born again and are revived by God's Spirit. Through faith, we can walk out of our Old Man and into our New Man. Just as our sin is forgiven, so too is our mental state under God's protection. As the New Man we can choose to live without the old trappings of all the negative stuff we tend to carry with us: fear, worry, anxiety, shame and more. Our soul, when surrendered to Him, allows us to overcome the world and all its trappings. Though our body is still mortal, our spirit is alive, and through the Holy Spirit that Yeshua has sent, we can overcome our mental weaknesses, worries and addictions.... and we will even receive a new physical body when Yeshua returns to earth.

It is only through Yeshua that we are free.

CHAPTER 5

What Yeshua is like and what he taught

Yeshua was a boy whose adopted father was a carpenter, so he grew up as a carpenter. Then, he went into full time ministry. He taught and performed miracles from the age of thirty to thirty-three. But he only did what his father, the Creator of the Universe, told him to do. Then he was arrested and his ministry seemed to be suspended. He was crucified, and buried. Then he was resurrected from the dead, and on a number of occasions to very many people who witnessed it, he proved he was a human being and not a ghost. He returned to Heaven, and sent the Holy Spirit to help us to live, love, laugh and grow into the persons we were created to be in the first place.

Better than describing him, here is what he said as recorded in the Bible.

Promises

"The thief does not come except to steal, and to kill, and to destroy. I have come that they may have life, and that they may have *it* more abundantly." (John 10:10)

"Come to me, all *you* who labour and are heavy laden, and I will give you rest. Take my yoke upon you and learn from me, for I am gentle and lowly in heart, and you will find rest for your souls. For my yoke *is* easy and my burden is light." (Matthew 11:28-30)

"For whoever desires to save his life will lose it, but whoever loses his life for my sake will find it." (Matthew 16:25)

"He who believes and is baptised will be saved; but he who does not believe will be condemned." (Mark 16:16)

"... but whoever drinks of the water that I shall give him will never thirst. But the water that I shall give him will become in him a fountain of water springing up into everlasting life." (John 4:14)

"He who believes in me, as the Scripture has said, out of his heart will flow rivers of living water." (John 7:38)

"If you abide in my word, you are my disciples indeed. And you shall know the truth, and the truth shall make you free." (John 31-32)

"For the Son of Man has come to save that which was lost." (Matthew 18:11)

Self-description including "I am..."

"I am the bread of life. He who comes to me shall never hunger, and he who believes in me shall never thirst." (John 6:35)

"I am the living bread which came down from heaven. If anyone eats of this bread, he will live forever; and the bread that I shall give is my flesh, which I shall give for the life of the world." (John 6:51)

"I am the true vine, and my Father is the vinedresser. Every branch in me that does not bear fruit He takes away; and every *branch* that bears fruit He prunes, that it may bear more fruit." (John 15:1-2)

"I am the light of the world. He who follows me shall not walk in darkness, but have the light of life." (John 8:12)

"He who believes in me, believes not in me but in Him who sent me. And he who sees me sees Him who sent me. I have come *as* a light into the world, that whoever believes in me should not abide in darkness. And if anyone hears my words and does not believe, I do not judge him; for I did not come to judge the world but to save the world. He who rejects me, and does not receive my words, has that which judges him—the word that I have spoken will judge him in the last day. For I have not spoken on my own *authority;* but the Father who sent me gave me a command, what I should say and what I should speak. And I know that His command is everlasting life. Therefore, whatever I speak, just as the Father has told me, so I speak." (John 12:44-50)

"Most assuredly, I say to you, before Abraham was, I am." (John 8:58)

On religious leaders of his time

"Therefore whatever they tell you to observe, *that* observe and do, but do not do according to their works; for they say, and do not do. For they bind heavy burdens, hard to bear, and lay *them* on men's shoulders; but they *themselves* will not move them with one of their fingers." (Matthew 23:3-4)

"Well did Isaiah prophesy of you hypocrites, as it is written:

'This people honours Me with *their* lips,
But their heart is far from Me.
And in vain they worship Me,
Teaching *as* doctrines the commandments of men."
(Mark 7:6-7)

His words to the people of Israel

"O Jerusalem, Jerusalem, the one who kills the prophets and stones those who are sent to her! How often I wanted to gather your children together, as a hen gathers her chicks under *her* wings, but you were not willing!" (Matthew 23:37)

God's love for mankind

"Consider the ravens, for they neither sow nor reap, which have neither storehouse nor barn; and God feeds them. Of how much more value are you than the birds?" (Luke 12:24)

About children

"Let the little children come to me, and do not forbid them; for of such is the kingdom of heaven." (Matthew 19:14)

Prayer

"When you pray, say:

Our Father in heaven,
Hallowed be Your name.

Your kingdom come.
Your will be done
On earth as *it is* in heaven.
Give us day by day our daily bread.
And forgive us our sins,
For we also forgive everyone who is indebted to us.
And do not lead us into temptation,
But deliver us from the evil one." (Luke 11:2-4)

"Father, forgive them, for they do not know what they do." (Luke 23:34)

Miracles

"If I do not do the works of my Father, do not believe me; but if I do, though you do not believe me, believe the works, that you may know and believe that the Father *is* in me, and I in Him." (John 10:37-38)

"Which is easier, to say to the paralytic, '*Your* sins are forgiven you,' or to say, 'Arise, take up your bed and walk'? But that you may know that the Son of Man has power on earth to forgive sins"—he said to the paralytic, "I say to you, arise, take up your bed, and go to your house." (Mark 2:9-11)

"For he said to him, 'Come out of the man, unclean spirit!'" (Mark 5:8)

"Daughter, your faith has made you well. Go in peace, and be healed of your affliction." (Mark 5:34)

"Why make this commotion and weep? The child is not dead, but sleeping.".... "Little girl, I say to you, arise." (see more detail at Mark 5:38-41)

"Why do you reason because you have no bread? Do you not yet perceive nor understand? Is your heart still hardened? Having eyes, do you not see? And having ears, do you not hear? And do you not remember? When I broke the five loaves for the five thousand [men], how many baskets full of fragments did you take up [afterward]?" (Mark 8:17-19)

"Launch out into the deep and let down your nets for a catch." (Luke 5:4)

"Rise, take up your bed and walk." (John 5:8)

"The things which are impossible with men are possible with God." (Luke 18:27)

His God-given Authority

"Most assuredly, I say to you, the Son can do nothing of Himself, but what he sees the Father do; for whatever He does, the Son also does in like manner." (John 5:19)

"But I have a greater witness than John's; for the works which the Father has given me to finish—the very works that I do—bear witness of me, that the Father has sent me." (John 5:36)

"You are from beneath; I am from above. You are of this world; I am not of this world." (John 8:23)

Instruction and teaching

"You shall love the Lord your God with all your heart, with all your soul, and with all your mind.' This is *the* first and great commandment. And *the* second *is* like it: 'You shall love your neighbour as yourself.' On these two commandments hang all the Law and the Prophets." (Matthew 22:37-40)

"Most assuredly, I say to you, unless one is born again, he cannot see the kingdom of God." (John 3:3)

"Judge not, that you be not judged. For with what judgment you judge, you will be judged; and with the measure you use, it will be measured back to you." (Matthew 7:1-2)

"When you are invited by anyone to a wedding feast, do not sit down in the best place, lest one more honourable than you be invited by him; and he who invited you and him come and say to you, 'Give place to this man,' and then you begin with shame to take the lowest place. But when you are invited, go and sit down in the lowest place, so that when he who invited you comes he may say to you, 'Friend, go up higher.' Then you will have glory in the presence of those who sit at the table with you. For whoever exalts himself will be humbled, and he who humbles himself will be exalted." (Luke 14:8-11)

"But I say to you who hear: Love your enemies, do good to those who hate you, bless those who curse you, and pray for those who spitefully use you." (Luke 6:27-28)

"Then he turned to the woman and said to Simon, 'Do you see this woman? I entered your house; you gave me no water for my feet, but she has washed my feet with her tears and wiped *them* with the hair of her head. You gave me no kiss, but this woman has not ceased to kiss my feet since the time I came in. You did not anoint my head with oil, but this woman has anointed my feet with fragrant oil. Therefore I say to you, her sins, which *are* many, are forgiven, for she loved much. But to whom little is forgiven, *the same* loves little.'" (Luke 7:44-47)

"Behold, I give you the authority to trample on serpents and scorpions, and over all the power of the enemy, and nothing shall by any means hurt you. Nevertheless do not rejoice in this, that the spirits are subject to you, but rather rejoice because your names are written in heaven." (Luke 10:19-20)

"And I will give you the keys of the kingdom of heaven, and whatever you bind on earth will be bound in heaven, and whatever you loose on earth will be loosed in heaven." (Matthew 16:19)

"Most assuredly, I say to you, he who believes in me, the works that I do he will do also; and greater *works* than these he will do, because I go to My Father. And whatever you ask in my name, that I will do, that the Father may be glorified in the Son." (John 14:12-13)

"...And as you go, preach, saying, 'The kingdom of heaven is at hand.' Heal the sick, cleanse the lepers, raise the dead, cast out demons. Freely you have received, freely give." (Matthew 10:7-8)

"For whoever desires to save his life will lose it, but whoever loses his life for my sake will save it. For what profit is it to a man if he gains the whole world, and is himself destroyed or lost? For whoever is ashamed of me and my words, of him the Son of Man will be ashamed when he comes in his *own* glory, and *in his* Father's, and of the holy angels." (Luke 9:24-26)

"Abide in me, and I in you. As the branch cannot bear fruit of itself, unless it abides in the vine, neither can you, unless you abide in me." (John 15:4)

"Go therefore and make disciples of all the nations, baptising them in the name of the Father and of the Son and of the Holy Spirit, teaching them to observe all things that I have commanded you; and lo, I am with you always, *even* to the end of the age." (Matthew 28:19-20)

About those who follow him

"You are the salt of the earth; but if the salt loses its flavour, how shall it be seasoned?" (Matthew 5:13)

Kingdom of God

"What is the kingdom of God like? And to what shall I compare it? It is like a mustard seed, which a man took and put in his garden; and it grew and became a large tree, and the birds of the air nested in its branches." (Luke 13:18-19)

Warnings

"When an unclean spirit goes out of a man, he goes through dry places, seeking rest, and finds none. Then he says, 'I will return to my house from which I came.' And when he comes, he finds *it* empty, swept, and put in order. Then he goes and takes with him seven other spirits more wicked than himself, and they enter and dwell there; and the last *state* of that man is worse than the first. So shall it also be with this wicked generation." (Matthew 12:43-45)

"So it will be at the end of the age. The angels will come forth, separate the wicked from among the just, and cast them into the furnace of fire. There will be wailing and gnashing of teeth." (Matthew 13:49-50)

"... then you will begin to say, 'We ate and drank in your presence, and you taught in our streets.' But he will say, 'I tell you I do not know you, where you are from. Depart from me, all you workers of iniquity.' There will be weeping and gnashing of teeth, when you see Abraham and Isaac and Jacob and all the prophets in the kingdom of God, and yourselves thrust out." (Luke 13:26-28)

"For then there will be great tribulation, such as has not been since the beginning of the world until this time, no, nor ever shall be." (Matthew 24:21)

Prophecies and the End of the World

"In My Father's house are many mansions; if *it were* not *so,* I would have told you. I go to prepare a place for you. And if I go and prepare a place for you, I will come again and receive you to myself; that where I am, *there* you may be also." (John 14:2-3)

"Assuredly I say to you, that in the regeneration, when the Son of Man sits on the throne of his glory, you who have followed me will also sit on twelve thrones, judging the twelve tribes of Israel. And everyone who has left houses or brothers or sisters or father or mother or wife or children or lands, for my name's sake, shall receive a hundredfold, and inherit eternal life. But many *who are* first will be last, and the last first." (Matthew 19:28-30)

"Then the sign of the Son of Man will appear in heaven, and then all the tribes of the earth will mourn, and they will see the Son of Man coming on the clouds of heaven with power and great glory. And he will send his angels with a great sound of a trumpet, and they will gather together his elect from the four winds, from one end of heaven to the other." (Matthew 24:30-31)

"When the Son of Man comes in his glory, and all the holy angels with him, then he will sit on the throne of his glory. All the nations will be gathered before him, and he will separate them one from another, as a shepherd divides *his* sheep from the goats." (Matthew 25:31-32)

During his suffering leading to arrest and death

"My soul is exceedingly sorrowful, even to death. Stay here and watch with me." (Matthew 26:38)

"And he said, 'Abba, Father, all things *are* possible for You. Take this cup away from me; nevertheless, not what I will, but what You *will.* '" (Mark 14:36)

"Father, if it is Your will, take this cup away from me; nevertheless not my will, but Yours, be done." (Luke 22:42)

"Assuredly, I say to you, today you will be with me in Paradise." (Luke 23:43)

Holy Spirit

"If you then, being evil, know how to give good gifts to your children, how much more will *your* heavenly Father give the Holy Spirit to those who ask Him!" (Luke 11:13)

"For the Holy Spirit will teach you in that very hour what you ought to say." (Luke 12:12)

"And I will pray the Father, and He will give you another Helper, that he may abide with you forever—the Spirit of truth, whom the world cannot receive, because it neither sees him nor knows him; but you know him, for he dwells with you and will be in you." (John 14:16-17)

"But the Helper, the Holy Spirit, whom the Father will send in my name, he will teach you all things, and bring to your remembrance all things that I said to you." (John 14:26)

"But when the Helper comes, whom I shall send to you from the Father, the Spirit of truth who proceeds from the Father, he will testify of me." (John 15:26)

"However, when he, the Spirit of truth, has come, he will guide you into all truth; for he will not speak on his own *authority,* but whatever he hears he will speak; and he will tell you things to come." (John 16:13)

Teaching using stories called 'parables'

"A certain man had two sons. And the younger of them said to *his* father, 'Father, give me the portion of goods that falls *to me.*' So he divided to them *his* livelihood. And not many days after, the younger son gathered all together, journeyed to a far country, and there wasted his possessions with prodigal living. But when he had spent all, there arose a severe famine in that land, and he began to be in want. Then he went and joined himself to a citizen of that country, and he sent him into his fields to feed swine. And he would gladly have filled his stomach with the pods that the swine ate, and no one gave him *anything.*

"But when he came to himself, he said, 'How many of my father's hired servants have bread enough and to spare, and I perish with hunger! I will arise and go to my father, and will say to him, "Father, I have sinned against heaven and before you, and I am no longer worthy to be called your son. Make me like one of your hired servants."'

"And he arose and came to his father. But when he was still a great way off, his father saw him and had compassion, and ran and fell on his neck and kissed him. And the son said to him, 'Father, I have sinned against heaven and in your sight, and am no longer worthy to be called your son.'

"But the father said to his servants, 'Bring out the best robe and put *it* on him, and put a ring on his hand and sandals on *his* feet. And bring the fatted calf here and kill *it,* and let us eat and be merry; for this my son was dead and is alive again; he was lost and is found.' And they began to be merry.

"Now his older son was in the field. And as he came and drew near to the house, he heard music and dancing. So he called one of the servants and asked what these things meant. And he said to him, 'Your brother has come, and because he has received him safe and sound, your father has killed the fatted calf.'

"But he was angry and would not go in. Therefore his father came out and pleaded with him. So he answered and said to *his* father, 'Lo, these many years I have been serving you; I never transgressed your commandment at any time; and yet you never gave me a young goat, that I might make merry with my friends. But as soon as this son of yours came, who has devoured your livelihood with harlots, you killed the fatted calf for him.'

"And he said to him, 'Son, you are always with me, and all that I have is yours. It was right that we should make merry and be glad, for your brother was dead and is alive again, and was lost and is found.'" (Luke 15:11-31)

After his resurrection from the dead

"Why are you troubled? And why do doubts arise in your hearts? Behold my hands and my feet, that it is I myself. Handle me and see, for a spirit does not have flesh and bones as you see I have." (Luke 24:38-39

"He said to them, 'So it is written, that the Messiah is to suffer and to rise from the dead on the third day, and that repentance for the removal of sins is to be proclaimed in his name to all nations, beginning from Jerusalem. You are witnesses of these things. And behold, I am sending the promise of my Father upon you; but you are to stay in the city until you are clothed with power from on high." (Luke 24:46-49 TLV)

Final words, not from Yeshua himself

The disciple John, who wrote the Gospel of John, from which many of the quotations above are found, finished his book with this statement,

"There are also many other things that Yeshua did. If all of them were to be written one by one, I suppose that not even the world itself will have room for the books being written!" (John 21:25 TLV)

Whether you call him by his Hebrew name, Yeshua, or his Greek/European/White Man name, Jesus, he was a man born of a virgin, who loved his Father, the Creator, and served Him so that we could all be reconciled back to Him. He died so that we all might have the opportunity to live: forgiven by Creator God, intimate with Father God, and free to be who He created us to be.

When his disciples ask him how to pray, he gave an example, and invited us all to call the Creator of the universe "Our Father."

CHAPTER 6

Who is the Holy Spirit?

The Holy Spirit brings life! The Holy Spirit is the Spirit who hovered over the earth at the time of Creation. He was the Spirit that brought life to Adam. He is the Spirit that makes us different from all other living creatures. He brings life to you and offers relationship to you. He is the comforter that Yeshua promised to send when he returned to the Father in Heaven. He is the Spirit of the Everlasting Father, Creator God.

Those who believe in Yeshua receive the Holy Spirit. The journey to following Yeshua is full of temptation and is not easy. It is the Holy Spirit who helps us to stay on the narrow path that leads to the Creator and to everlasting life.

When any person believes the message about Yeshua and wants to follow him, he receives the Holy Spirit. The Holy Spirit is that which emanates from God that is within those of us who have given our lives to Jesus the Saviour. The Holy Spirit convicts us of sin, leads us to truth, and is the power and presence of God. I wonder: those missionaries who preached in the name of Jesus and yet condemned other cultures, did they carry within them the Holy Spirit? Was it cruelty or ignorance that prejudiced them?

Receiving the Holy Spirit

Anyone who follows Yeshua receives this Holy Spirit that revives the otherwise dead spirit we were born with. Remember when God breathed into Adam and gave him His spirit? When Adam rebelled, the spirit within him died. All those of the following generations were born without a living spirit, because they were descended from Adam. But four thousand years after Adam, God made a way for the human spirit once again to be revived.

From that time to this, the Holy Spirit lives within anyone who follows Yeshua.

Holy Spirit and Great Spirit

I have wondered about the identity of this Holy Spirit. I have often wondered: Did God reveal Himself as the Creator many centuries ago to the First Nations people, and is the Great Spirit who is known among the First Nations people today one and the same Holy Spirit?

The Bible says, "Beloved, do not believe every spirit, but test the spirits, whether they are of God; because many false prophets have gone out into the world. By this you know the Spirit of God: Every spirit that confesses that Jesus Christ has come in the flesh is of God, and every spirit that does not confess that Jesus Christ has come in the flesh is not of God. And this is the *spirit* of the Antichrist, which you have heard was coming, and is now already in the world." (1 John 4:1-3)

In my own mind, I haven't reconciled if the Great Spirit and the Holy Spirit are one and the same, because I do not know enough about the Great Spirit. I do believe though, that as a First Nations person seeks Truth, the identity of the Great Spirit, and whether he is one and the same as the Holy Spirit, will be revealed.

Traditional First Nations people recognise the Creator of the Universe. They know of the Great Spirit. But what about the Holy Spirit? Maybe the Great Spirit and the Holy Spirit are one and the same, though First Nations tradition and culture have not recognised that the Spirit was actually sent by Yeshua to draw us closer to him.

Only One Spirit of God

We know there are many spirits, but only the Holy Spirit draws us toward Creator God. There are other clever spirits that actually work for the devil, and want to draw us away from God, because the devil and God are arch enemies.

The Holy Spirit is the spirit of life.

Let me share more of what I know about the Holy Spirit so you can determine whether the Great Spirit that you know is the same spirit as God's Holy Spirit.

The Holy Spirit does not keep his distance from me, but rather, he comforts me when I am hurting and convicts me (shows me when I do wrong, although he never condemns me) of my wrong-doing. He is the helper who counsels me, and draws me towards the Creator. He lives within me and did so the minute I decided to follow Yeshua. He will do the same for you.

"Peter said to them, 'Repent, and let each of you be immersed in the name of Messiah Yeshua for the removal of your sins, and you will receive the gift of the Ruach ha-Kodesh'(Holy Spirit)" (Acts 2:38 TLV)

John 3:16 says, "For God so loved the world that He gave His only begotten son, that whoever believes in him should not perish but have everlasting life." It is through the Holy Spirit that everlasting life is possible.

Does this Holy Spirit match the identity of the Great Spirit? If not, may I invite you to discover more about the most powerful and loving spirit in the universe?

This Holy Spirit gives freely, connects us to God and does not require worship or sacrifice

Human beings want to know God — the Creator. Everyone is born knowing of His existence.

"For since the creation of the world His invisible attributes are clearly seen, being understood by the things that are made, even His eternal power and Godhead, so that they are without excuse, because, although they knew God, they did not glorify Him as God, nor were thankful, but became futile in their thoughts, and their foolish hearts were darkened." (Romans 1:20-21)

God has put the knowledge of Himself within every person. Some people are angry with Him because He won't come to them on their terms, and so they deny His existence. But deep within us all we are born knowing God exists.

Spirit of Religion is not the Holy Spirit

All around the world and throughout history, people have tried to reach God through their own ways. You've heard of the Tower of Babel? People built a tower to try to reach Heaven so they could be like God.

There is history around the world about people trying to worship and appease "the gods".

You've heard of world religions? There are many. To name a few, there is: Hindu, Sikh, Buddist, Catholic, Orthodox, Islam, Tao, Ancestral Worship, Animist, Confucius. Religion is man-made. Even a Christian religion can stir up trouble, because it can stir up demons. Without intending to, often people have worshipped demons, thinking they are worshipping God. Demons bind us, control us, hate us, hate God, cause us to sin, and can drive us to insanity.

Evil Spirits and demon possession can provoke us to Insanity

In Mark chapter 5 there is one account of a man so full of demons he's given the name Legion (meaning one thousand),

"As soon as Yeshua got out of the boat, a man from the graveyard with an unclean spirit met him. He lived among the tombs, and no one could restrain him anymore, even with a chain. For he had often been bound with shackles and chains, but the chains had been ripped apart by him and the shackles broken. No one was strong enough to tame him. And through it all, night and day, at the graveyard and in the mountains, he kept screaming and gashing himself with stones. When he saw Yeshua from a distance, he ran and bowed down before him. Crying out with a loud voice, he said, 'What's between you and me, Yeshua, Ben El Elyon? I'm warning you, in the name of God, do not torment me!' For Yeshua had said to him, 'Come out of the man, you unclean spirit!' Then Yeshua began questioning him, 'What is your name?' And he answered, 'My name is Legion, for we are many.'"

As the account in the Bible continues, Yeshua does cast out the demons from the man, sends them into a heard of pigs, which then throw themselves over a cliff. The man is now sane, the townspeople send Yeshua away, and so ends one account of what the power of demons can do... and what the power of God can do through Yeshua by the Holy Spirit.

Spiritual Freedom

We can be free from demons through Yeshua. The power of the Holy Spirit can help us to live free.

Some people offer sacrifices in their religion. But Yeshua paid the sacrifice for everyone and with the help of the Holy Spirit we can live the life God intends for us, free from having to sacrifice any longer. Instead of offering sacrifice we can thank and praise God for all He has done to draw us to Himself again.

Holy Spirit helps us to trust God and helps us to live free

God wants us to worship Him, but not through sacrifice. He wants us to trust Him and to put our faith in Him. When we trust Him and obey His Law of Love, we are equipped with the Holy Spirit to fight against temptation and sin.

"The sacrifices of God are a broken spirit, A broken and a contrite heart— These, O God, You will not despise" (Psalm 51:17) because Yeshua is the sacrifice.

To have a broken heart is to realise we are not capable of living right without God. We become humble and willing to allow Him to come into our lives so we can live right and inherit everlasting life. The pain of this broken heart does not last… it isn't like living with the loss of or break up from a loved one. Rather, it is temporary - a sense that we need God. The Holy Spirit draws us to God. Then the pain can be healed and the need fulfilled.

What is the Holy Spirit like?

I know the Holy Spirit. His character is goodness, kindness, gentleness, love, joy, peace, faithfulness, patience and self control, and offers these same traits to us. (Galatians 5:22-23)

God is love. We see this through Yeshua's behaviour as well as the words he says:

"Do not think that I came to destroy the Law or the Prophets. I did not come to destroy but to fulfil." (Matthew 5:17)

"So he answered and said, 'You shall love the Lord your God with all your heart, with all your soul, with all your strength, and with all your mind,' and 'your neighbour as yourself.'" (Luke 10:27)

Does your understanding of the Great Spirit lead you to worship the Creator and draw closer to a loving heavenly Father Who knows and cares for you? That's what the Holy Spirit does.

What we know of the Holy Spirit

The Holy Spirit helps us to see where we are far from God and draws us closer. He convicts us of sin, but he never, never condemns us.

"Therefore, there is now no condemnation for those who are in Messiah Yeshua. For the law of the Spirit of life in Messiah Yeshua has set you free from the law of sin and death." (Romans 8:1-2 TLV)

The Holy Spirit is Gentle

When Joseph, the fiancé of the virgin Miriam — Mary — learned of her pregnancy, he was conflicted. He had never had sex with her and so he knew he was not the father. He didn't want to marry her. And yet he did not wish her to be stoned to death, the penalty for a woman who had sex out of wedlock.

Then an angel spoke to him in a dream saying, "Joseph, son of David, do not be afraid to take to you Mary your wife, for that which is conceived in her is of the Holy Spirit." (Matthew 1:20b)

Father God, Creator of the universe, ensured life was in the womb of an innocent girl through His spirit. He brought forth a life that would rescue the world from its evil self, and then He made sure the girl would be honoured and not punished.

What if the Great Spirit is Holy

If the Great Spirit is full of the goodness of the Creator, that is wonderful! Through Yeshua, you can receive God's Spirit personally.

What if the Great Spirit is not Holy

However, if your understanding of the Great Spirit leads you to worship him separately from God, or threatens, intimidates, or encourages you to do evil, if he leads you towards idols or bad behaviour such as debauchery, addiction, lust, cursing or other sins, or if he condemns you and shames you, or threatens you, he is not one with the Holy Spirit. If he makes you afraid, he is not of God. He is not one with Creator God and you do not need to worship or follow his mistaken identity. The Holy Spirit can free you from this spirit if he is an imposter.

What does this new life, which includes the Holy Spirit, offer?

Freedom. It is not rules, regulations, or culture. Those are aspects of religion! It is not sacrifice. Yeshau is the sacrifice for us. It is freedom, and with it the dignity of responsibility. The Holy Spirit of the Creator God offers us the power and presence to live free, to live in love, goodness, and kindness; it overcomes bitterness, unforgiveness, and addiction. It does not do evil nor call for evil to be inflicted on others. It does not curse but brings life.

Life. It was Yeshua who was conceived by the spirit of the Creator of the Universe. The spirit is life-giving. He gave life to Yeshua and he offers life to you and me.

No Condemnation, No Demons

The Holy Spirit is pure and holy. Nothing of the Holy Spirit condemns or causes harm, shame or fear. He draws us to God, to worship Him and to receive His goodness and love.

From the beginning of time, we have been called to worship the Creator personally and directly, with nothing and no one between us and Him. No image or symbol of the Creator is necessary. There is a direct line from us to Him; the Holy Spirit acts like a connection wire, linking us to the Father.

One of the reasons I emphasise this is so we are not tricked into worshipping demons, which like to imitate the supernatural God, and to contort our relationship with Him. Demons are at war with the Creator and want to defeat Him by defeating us.

Holy Spirit helps us in our transformation to new life

In the Gospel of John, which is one of the books in the Bible, the role the Holy Spirit plays in this transformation to new life is explained. This is for anyone who believes,

"Yeshua answered, 'Amen, amen I tell you, unless one is born of water and spirit, he cannot enter the kingdom of God. What is born of the flesh is flesh, and what is born of the Spirit is spirit. Do not be surprised that I said to you, 'You all must be born from above.' The wind blows where it wishes and you hear its sound, but you do not know where it comes from or where it goes. So it is with everyone born of the Spirit.'" (John 3:5-8 TLV)

Salvation is in an instant. Sometimes our new life with Yeshua changes us immediately, while for others of us change takes more time. Either way, Holy Spirit brings life to anyone who chooses to believe and follow Yeshua.

The Spirit is Life Forever

The White Man calls the Father of Creation God and Lord. The Hebrew uses the name Yehova and Adonai. There is so much the White Man has translated; he has wiped out much of the Hebrew heritage that was orchestrated by God. But although the White Man has made many mistakes, God has forgiven him and the Truth remains the same: The Creator's way to salvation and new life is through the life, death and resurrection of a Jewish person named Yeshua. And it is by the power of the Holy Spirit, the same spirit who hovered over the Universe at creation and the same spirit who made a virgin pregnant, that we can have freedom in this life and an everlasting life too.

If this life-giving identity is a reflection of the Great Spirit, then this is more about the Great Spirit whom you already identify.

If this is not the identity of the Great Spirit, then I introduce you to the Holy Spirit, who has much greater power than any other spirit, just as the Creator has much greater power over any other god invented by man.

White Man's Mistakes: Did the White Man have the Holy Spirit?

God has revealed His Truth through the Bible but the understanding of the Bible has been gradual, and it is over centuries that we have come to understand God's Word more and more. From the early years of Christianity, much was lost and is only gradually returning to us. In particular, we have not had full understanding of the Holy Spirit.

The Bible promises that all who are born again receive the Holy Spirit. But for many there is a gap between our mental understanding and our supernatural experience. The Old Man likes to keep control although the New Man is surrendered. Sometimes the Old Man, with pride and his own desire to honour God his way, and all sorts of other undesirable qualities, has not done what the Spirit would want but rather he clings onto what he wants to do himself. Yeshua teaches we are to die to our own desires, but sometimes that takes a while to happen. In the meantime, and throughout history, many people did horrible things "in the name of Jesus." Sadly, it drew people away from God and God got the blame for mankind's ignorance, stupidity and its tendency to judge others.

"For we know that the law is spiritual, but I am carnal, sold under sin. For what I am doing, I do not understand. For what I will to do, that I do not practice; but what I hate, that I do." (Romans 7:14-15)

The White Man does not have authority over the Bible or the Truth. He has done his best to understand and to communicate this truth, in order to honour the Great Commission that Yeshua instructed before he returned to the Father.

"And he said to them, 'Go into all the world and preach the gospel to every creature.'" (Mark 16:15)

Those telling others about Yeshua may have meant well, though many did not it do it God's way. The White Man's Gospel has taken many twists and turns over the centuries. Now we are in a time when many believers of Jesus are recognising the Hebrew origins and are seeing more of the Truth of Messiah Yeshua.

Jewish Awakening

Like the First Nations people, Hebrews have their history of joy and sorrow. The Jews — and not the White

Man — are God's chosen people, which is why they told the Creator's story through the Bible (called Torah* in Hebrew).

Although the Hebrew people rejected their Messiah, and cursed themselves, their behaviour fulfilled prophecies from the Bible,

"He is despised and rejected by men, A man of sorrows and acquainted with grief. And we hid, as it were, our faces from him; he was despised, and we did not esteem him." (Isaiah 53:3)

And now many Jewish people are coming to recognise their Messiah and are even helping Gentile believers to better understand a greater scope of who the Creator of the Universe is.

Gospel reading: Good News from the Bible

Just like God breathed into Adam and gave him His spirit, the Holy Bible has the breath of God within it. The Holy Spirit imparted the words to be written in the Bible so that we would have God's Truth.

If you read the entire books of Matthew and John in the Bible, you will get a much more full and complete picture of God's intention for us. He sent Yeshua to accomplish more than I can convey in this booklet. Yeshua is a model of God, whose kindness knows no equal; his goodness is incomparable. And God's power in Yeshua gave him the authority to heal. It is through Yeshua's death and resurrection that our faith saves our spirit from eternal death.

Can the Great Spirit revive your spirit? The Holy Spirit can.

The White Man has made many mistakes over the centuries, both in understanding the Gospel of Yeshua, and in delivering it. But the Gospel — the message of life, love and hope from Father Creator God — is true. Let neither the truth nor your understanding of God be tainted or distorted by the wrong-doings of Christians of the past.

No Culture Contest

You don't need to reject your Creator God to know Yeshua. You can have relationship with Him through the Holy Spirit. It is only because of Yeshua's sacrifice that you can have this unique restoration to relationship with the Creator and this new life He offers to any who believe.

"Yeshua said to him, "I am the way, the truth, and the life! No one comes to the Father except through Me.'" (John 14:6 TLV)

Be assured, giving your life to Yeshua does not change your culture. It does offer to transform the quality of your existence on earth and forever, if you allow it to.

When you surrender your life to Yeshua, the Spirit of the Creator will transform that which in His eyes needs to be transformed, so that you will be free as Yeshua is free. Some of your ways — your perceptions, your attitudes, your sorrows — will go. But that is the same for all who follow Yeshua, including the White Man, including me.** God's ways are not our ways, but His way through Yeshua is the only way that brings life, now and forever.

Choose life, that you might have it more abundantly. Choose Yeshua because he is the way to that life. Choose the one true path to the Father, Creator of the heavens and the earth, so that by His Spirit you will be set free from all man-made confusion and from spiritual death. Choose Yeshua and by the Holy Spirit, you will have new life.

* The Hebrew Bible includes only the Old Testament, the books from Genesis to Malachi.

** In my life there have been some things about myself I could not stand! One by one, God is removing those from me, with my cooperation, and so I am a much nicer person and one I like much more!:)

CHAPTER 7

How do I receive Yeshua?
What should I expect as a result?

Accepting Yeshua and following him isn't actually something we do all by ourselves. The faith to believe comes from God.

"Faith comes by hearing and hearing by the Word of God." (Romans 10:17)

Receive by asking and believing... It's that simple

With the desire to follow him, simply talk to him and tell him what you want to do. Ask him to forgive all your past mistakes and accept his forgiveness. Invite the Holy Spirit to come into your life; believe that he does, and allow him to begin to move within you, comforting you, healing you, showing you the way to follow Yeshua. There will be some things you'll have to give up, if you want to be whole and well; let those things go so that you can receive freedom and peace. Otherwise, they will hold you back.

You can ask for this gift of a new life and you can expect God to give it to you. Information from God's Word, the Bible, will help to build your faith. I have been quoting information from the Bible in this book to give you the chance to see what it says, this is an ancient document which has been tested and proven to be accurate many times over.

I have not said anything that isn't also stated in the Bible, and nothing I've not experienced first hand as the truth in my own life.

Learn from the Bible, where you'll find help to build your belief. You can even read it on-line for free.

Walking with Yeshua is exciting and challenging, but the Holy Spirit is with you, within you to help you. If you want to follow Yeshua, you can. It isn't done by following rules and regulations, but by loving him and allowing him to love you. Being with others who also follow him will help you a lot. Who you spend time with can help or hurt you. "Do not be deceived! 'Evil company corrupts good habits.'" (1 Corinthians 15:33)

Being with other believers is helpful as you seek to grow in your walk with Yeshua. "Iron sharpens iron"; if you are with others who are seeking to grow spiritually, you will all grow together: in prayer, in study, in character. "Again I say to you that if two of you agree on earth concerning any-thing that they ask, it will be done for them by My Father in heaven." (Matthew 18:19)

Knowing the Scriptures Builds Your Faith

"For the word of God is living and powerful, and sharper than any two-edged sword, piercing even to the division of soul and spirit, and of joints and marrow, and is a discerner of the thoughts and intents of the heart." (Hebrews 4:12)

Yeshua said he fulfilled a prophecy given hundreds of years before his birth. The description of how he declared himself is recorded in Luke,

"So he [Yeshua] came to Nazareth, where he had been brought up. And as his custom was, he went into the synagogue on the Sabbath day, and stood up to read. And he was handed the book of the prophet Isaiah. And when he had opened the book, he found the place where it was written:

"'The Spirit of the LORD *is* upon me,
Because he has anointed me
To preach the gospel to *the* poor;
He has sent me to heal the broken hearted,
To proclaim liberty to *the* captives
And recovery of sight to *the* blind,
To set at liberty those who are oppressed;
To proclaim the acceptable year of the LORD.'

Then he closed the book, and gave *it* back to the attendant and sat down. And the eyes of all who were in the synagogue were fixed on him. And he began to say to them, 'Today this Scripture is fulfilled in your hearing.'" (Luke 4:17-21)

Unless you think Yeshua had the character of a liar or a person who was delusional, you'll know what he said is true. Having the knowledge of this scripture will help you when times of doubt try to creep into your mind.

Faith doesn't come from our own efforts

Faith to believe that Yeshua is who he claimed to be is a gift from God that we can ask for.

"For by grace you have been saved through faith, and that not of yourselves; *it is* the gift of God," (Ephesians 2:8)

What about having doubts

It's okay to have doubts and questions. God has given us a mind to use to think things through and make decisions. You can ask Him any questions and expect Him to answer.

"If you then, being evil, know how to give good gifts to your children, how much more will your Father who is in heaven give good things to those who ask Him." (Matthew 7:11)

How to behave

There isn't a religious way to behave when you follow Yeshua. He died to set us free. However, we are called and empowered to love as he loves us, and that will help us to behave in a way that is life-giving to ourselves and to others.

"Concerning His Son,
  He came into being
    from the seed of David
      according to the flesh.
      He was appointed
        Ben-Elohim
      in power
    according to the Ruach of holiness,
  by the resurrection from the dead.
He is Messiah Yeshua our Lord.

Through him we have received grace and the office of emissary, to bring about obedience of faith among all the nations on behalf of his name." (Romans 1:3-5 TLV))

Having the Peace of God which passes all understanding

And faith gives us peace with God, whom Yeshua teaches us to call Father.

"Therefore, having been made righteous by trusting, we have Shalom (peace) with God through our Lord Yeshua the Messiah." (Romans 5:1 TLV)

Walking in the Spirit of God

The Spirit of God can enable us to have confidence in our new life and joy. We can overcome any past behaviour that is damaging, hurtful or fearful, with God's help and the desire to overcome.

"I can do all things through Messiah who strengthens me." (Philippians 4:13 TLV)

Through faith we are born again. We confess to Yeshua our sin (rebellion against God) and our need for him, and say we want to follow him. We receive the Holy Spirit as it says,

"In order that through Messiah Yeshua the blessing of Abraham might come to the Gentiles, so we might receive the promise of the Ruach through trusting faith." (Galatians 3:14 TLV)

Behaviour and Attitude

Once we have given our lives to Jesus, there are not rules – except for the rule of love! Love covers the Ten Commandments and traditions, cultures, and expectations.

There are consequences of our actions, right or wrong, which will help or hinder our walk of faith and our joy, which I'll explain more in the final chapter.

What did Yeshua say about rules, law and love?

"Do not think that I came to destroy the Law or the Prophets. I did not come to destroy but to fulfil." (Matthew 5:17)

How do we fulfil the Law and the Prophets?

"A new commandment I give to you, that you love one another; as I have loved you, that you also love one another." (John 13:34)

Yeshua defines love,

"Greater love has no one than this, than to lay down one's life for his friends." (John 15:13)

Take Care of Yourself

That you respect your body, mind and spirit is important to God,

"Or do you not know that your body is the temple of the Holy Spirit who is in you, whom you have from God, and you are not your own? For you were bought at a price; therefore glorify God in your body and in your spirit, which are God's." (1Corinthians 6:19-20)

"What shall we say then? Shall we continue in sin that grace may abound? Certainly not! How shall we who died to sin live any longer in it?" (Romans 6:1)

Outside of Faith is Religion

Outside this expression of love and faith is culture, expectation and rules. Human beings feel safer with rules, but actually, we are free from sin and death — and rules — when we commit our lives to Yeshua. There is a lot of guidance given throughout the letters in the New Testament of the Bible (the books from Romans onwards). These were written as the church was developing. When we follow this guidance, it helps us to grow to be more like Yeshua; he was and is at peace with himself, not anxious or fearful or trapped. But there is not a set of rules to follow that will bring us closer to God. Following Yeshua is actually what sets us free from fear and rules, and helps us to draw closer to God who is our wonderful Father.

For those of us who have sought God and are born again, we find the right way to live as we spend time with Him in prayer. Reading the Word that God has given us helps us with our questions; the Bible is spiritual food. Spending time with other believers helps us to defend ourselves against the enemy – the devil — who comes to seek and to destroy our confidence and faith in God. Worshipping God – not His creation but Him alone and directly – will help us to shed the past ways of thinking and acting that are hurtful to ourselves and others, and to grow more like Him.

There are battles ahead to fight. They are different from past battles before we were born again, but battles nevertheless.

"For we do not wrestle against flesh and blood, but against principalities, against powers, against the rulers of the darkness of this age, against spiritual *hosts* of wickedness in the heavenly *places*." (Ephesians 6:12)

We have to turn our back against our flesh (our will, urgings and temptations), against the world (attractions and distractions) and the devil, who is Satan, who hates God and wants us to worship any but the one true Creator God. So, following Yeshua is not without challenges, but it is true freedom and the way to joy, peace and hope. With faith in Yeshua and the help of the Holy Spirit, we can live. This New Man leaves the past wounds and failings behind.

Baptism

"Then Yeshua came from the Galilee to John, to be immersed by him in the Jordan. But John tried to prevent Him, saying, "I need to be immersed by you, and you are coming to me?" But Yeshua responded, "Let it happen now, for in this way it is fitting for us to fulfill all righteousness." So John yielded to him. After being immersed, Yeshua rose up out of the water; and behold, the heavens were opened to him, and he saw the Ruach Elohim (Holy Spirit) descending like a dove and coming upon him. And behold, a voice from the heavens said, "This is My Son, whom I love; with Him I am well pleased!"" (Matthew 3:13-17 TLV)

Since Yeshua modelled baptism (full immersion in water as an act of repentance), it's a blessing and an opportunity available to us also.

Later in Acts 2:38, after Yeshua's return to the Father in Heaven, it is recorded,

"Peter said to them, "Repent, and let each of you be immersed in the name of Messiah Yeshua for the removal of your sins, and you will receive the gift of the Ruach ha-Kodesh.'" (TLV)

While baptism is something we do as a choice that shows our commitment to Yeshua, there is further reason for it. Spiritually, it also acts to seal our faith and gives us more supernatural authority over our enemy the devil, who seeks to destroy our faith and our relationship with God, our peace and joy, and our assurance of God's love.

We can expect love, joy, peace, goodness, kindness, gentleness, faithfulness, patience, and self-control from the Holy Spirit; but we can also expect opposition from the devil. The reason to grow in Christ when we become *saved* is to help us to win the battles that will come from this enemy. Our prayers, our understanding of the authority we have through Yeshua, our family of Christians praying for us, and with us: all these things help us to defeat the enemy's efforts to entrap us in pain, grief, control, none of which is *of heaven*.

The Supernatural

Supernatural experience is also a circumstance among God's family. There is no reason to think that God does not heal and deliver today by His Holy Spirit, just as He did with Yeshua and his disciples. Prophecy too still occurs today.

"Most assuredly, I say to you, he who believes in me, the works that I do he will do also; and greater *works* than these he will do, because I go to My Father." (John 14:12)

Sometimes people make mistakes; any supernatural activity should match what is in the Bible and can be tested by God's Word. You can pray for His help and supernatural revelation and understanding in these circumstances.

Yeshua performed miracles, but he only did that which the Father called him to do. As we follow God and obey Him, He will call upon us. He knows us, He sees clearly who we are and who He created us to be,

"O LORD, You have searched me and known *me.*
You know my sitting down and my rising up;
You understand my thought afar off.
You comprehend my path and my lying down,
And are acquainted with all my ways.
For *there is* not a word on my tongue,
But behold, O LORD, You know it altogether."
(Psalm 139:1-4)

Life following Yeshua as a new believer is a journey. The journey will not end until our natural death and union with God in heaven.

The journey never promises freedom from suffering or disappointment, but it does promise the strength to overcome, and joy in any circumstance.

Remember, "I can do all things through Christ who strengthens me." (Philippians 4:13) This is one bedrock scripture. You'll find it really useful to memorise it and pray it as you go through difficult moments in your journey.

Thinking with a Renewed Mind
One of our tasks is to allow God to transform our thinking from the Old Man to the New Man thinking.

"I beseech you therefore, brethren, by the mercies of God, that you present your bodies a living sacrifice, holy, acceptable to God, *which is* your reasonable service. And do not be conformed to this world, but be transformed by the renewing of your mind, that you may prove what *is* that good and acceptable and perfect will of God." (Romans 12:1-2)

Turning from the Past

The Old Man that you were may be riddled with low self-esteem, anxiety or fear. A weakness some of us have is to manipulate or to scheme in order to fill a need for love. But we have been forgiven for our past and can walk in new life. The New Man has given Yeshua all of the old ways of thinking and can choose to ignore them. Empowered by the Holy Spirit and covered in love, with the glory of God as our rearguard (ref Isaiah 58:8), we can walk in this new life with God our Father, confident that whatever comes in our path is God's opportunity to teach us to be more like Him. He never leaves us or forsakes us. He is aware of our shortcomings, weaknesses and the things that tempt us. But He teaches us, even through our ordinary life experiences, how to overcome.

We can choose to face and resist the devil, and he will flee. We can flee from temptation and turn our backs on the former, lifeless habits. We cannot do this in our own strength. But with God's Holy Spirit to help us, and the prayers of other saints, all things can be overcome.

Here is the basic fact: that which is not Yeshua is dead; it died when Adam sinned. Real life comes from God the

Father, and we that receive Yeshua/Jesus Christ have a chance to live that life as God intended, full of the Spirit of God and full of wholesome, free life. As we surround ourselves with God's truth, love and life, we overcome the world, sin and the death. As we choose the New Man, we choose life.

"The thief does not come except to steal, and to kill, and to destroy. I [Yeshua] have come that they may have life, and that they may have *it* more abundantly." (John 10:10 TLV)

CHAPTER 8

Can I walk with Yeshua and keep my Cultural Identity?

God has made you a unique person with a unique purpose in a special culture. You are not your culture, nor another man's culture. There is nothing that is unclean or that should be denied, unless you have made it of greater importance to you than is God, or it causes someone else to be confused or drawn away from God.

Yeshua said, "Not what goes into the mouth defiles a man; but what comes out of the mouth, this defiles a man." (Matthew 15:11) That is taken to mean, whereas in earlier times certain foods were forbidden in the Jewish culture, now under Yeshua, the law is fulfilled in love, and those foods are not what is so important to God, but what comes out from inside of us – what we say and how we behave toward others – reveals our hearts toward them and God. It is the state of our hearts that matters most to God.

This applies to issues of culture.

Man-made is Flawed

Everything man-made is flawed. That includes every culture, with the exception of the original Hebrew culture that was designed by God, but which has since been revised by man.

Throughout the New Testament (the second half of the Bible that begins with Yeshua's birth in the Book of Matthew) it is made clear that activities and lifestyles which harm others or damage your own body are ungodly; but traditions and cultures in themselves are not an issue with the Lord. And God helps us through any damage we've done in the past to ourselves or to others, whether intentional or accidental.

"Trust in the LORD* with all your heart,
And lean not on your own understanding;
In all your ways acknowledge Him,
And He shall direct your paths." (Proverbs 3:5-6)

Overcoming Evil with Good is a Process

Through prayer and surrender to God's love and authority, you will be able to find what is pure and good in your culture and what is destructive. The boundaries for our behaviour and activity depend upon our relationship with the Father God, with our own spiritual maturity, and how we might influence others toward or away from what is godly (safe, helpful, healing, and holy).

"All things are lawful for me, but not all things are helpful; all things are lawful for me, but not all things edify. Let no one seek his own, but each one the other's *well-being.*" (1 Corinthians 8:23-24)

The biggest key to walking closely with God is allowing the Old Man to be dead, because he *is* dead and doesn't warrant any attention. To let the New Man, who is godly, rise up in you, is what is strengthening and wonderful, joyful and holy. This is not easy because the Old Man wants attention, but it is possible. It's a process. Ignore the old, embrace the new as you embrace Yeshua. That is where you'll find new life!

As you grow in faith, you will not want a less mature believer to 'stumble' because of your behavior, will you? Out of love for others, you may have to lay aside some of your cultural activities temporarily, so that others are able to grow. Perhaps at a later time – in different circumstances, or when you are on your own – you may take part in cultural activities that would otherwise put at risk another's relationship with or understanding of the Creator God.

The Ten Commandments

Between the time of Abraham and Yeshua, there was the development of the Jewish nation, beginning with Moses leading the Hebrews from captivity to freedom. (Do you remember the story of the parting of the Red Sea?) At this time, to protect the people, God gave guidelines called The Ten Commandments, laws for the new nation so that they would be different from all other nations:

> "2 "I *am* the LORD your God, who brought you out of the land of Egypt, out of the house of bondage.
>
> 3 "You shall have no other gods before Me.
>
> 4 "You shall not make for yourself a carved image— any likeness *of anything* that *is* in heaven above, or that

is in the earth beneath, or that *is* in the water under the earth; ⁵ you shall not bow down to them nor serve them. For I, the Lᴏʀᴅ your God, *am* a jealous God, visiting the iniquity of the fathers upon the children to the third and fourth *generations* of those who hate Me, ⁶ but showing mercy to thousands, to those who love Me and keep My commandments.

⁷ "You shall not take the name of the Lᴏʀᴅ your God in vain, for the Lᴏʀᴅ will not hold *him* guiltless who takes His name in vain.

⁸ "Remember the Sabbath day, to keep it holy. ⁹ Six days you shall labour and do all your work, ¹⁰ but the seventh day *is* the Sabbath of the Lᴏʀᴅ your God. *In it* you shall do no work: you, nor your son, nor your daughter, nor your male servant, nor your female servant, nor your cattle, nor your stranger who *is* within your gates. ¹¹ For *in* six days the Lᴏʀᴅ made the heavens and the earth, the sea, and all that *is* in them, and rested the seventh day. Therefore the Lᴏʀᴅ blessed the Sabbath day and hallowed it.

¹² "Honour your father and your mother, that your days may be long upon the land which the Lᴏʀᴅ your God is giving you.

¹³ "You shall not murder.

¹⁴ "You shall not commit adultery.

¹⁵ "You shall not steal.

¹⁶ "You shall not bear false witness against your neighbour.

[17] "You shall not covet your neighbour's house; you shall not covet your neighbour's wife, nor his male servant, nor his female servant, nor his ox, nor his donkey, nor anything that *is* your neighbour's." (Exodus 20:2-17)

These are good laws, but they are completed through the love that Yeshua teaches and offers: love of God first, and then love of others. If a society follows the Ten Commandments, it is a safer society in every way than a society that does not. But actually, if we are followers of Yeshua, the commandments will be fulfilled as we do God's will by His Holy Spirit. We don't have to strive to obey but rather when we love, we live.

Set Free from Law…except the Law of Love

The truth is that the Lord Jesus has set you free from the law of sin and death; the Lord has bought for you an abundance of life and freedom. However, you are under one law – that of love. Acting in freedom without regard for the effect it will have on others, is not acting in love.

So, for example, if attending a Pow Wow will enable you to worship the LORD Creator God in spirit and in truth, that is wonderful.

But what if attending that Pow Wow will cause another person to be confused about Yeshua? Perhaps (s)he is looking at you for godly guidance. What if a Pow Wow would cause this friend to be drawn away from God? Perhaps they only understand a Pow Wow as a spiritual activity of native tradition that is a form of worship to a god contrary to the God and Father of creation and of Yeshua.

Your involvement in the Pow Wow may prevent him from embracing true relationship with Yeshua. So actually, by loving the other person and wanting him to be closer to God, avoiding the Pow Wow for the time being, might seem to be the more loving thing to do.

History: First Nations Worship the Creator God

However, there is much proof that aboriginal groups know and worship God through their traditions.

There is an interesting story about a Native American group playing 120 Drums and being overheard by some Rabbis (Jewish spiritual leaders). The drummers were stopped and asked, "Where did you get that music?" The answer was that the music had been passed down for generations – chants that they did not understand themselves but which they performed as part of their celebrations.

The Rabbis said that the musical chants were high Hebrew, singing praises to God.

How could the Native Americans have known the language? They did not. But somewhere in their culture it had been given to them. (This from an interview between Dr Mark Chironna and John Paul Jackson on TBN, aired September 10th, 2009, posted on You Tube at https://www.youtube.com/watch?v=nhp6M0a9ZA8)

You don't need to doubt that the LORD does amazing things, or that the indigenous people around the world are a part of this. Father God loves all of His people and we are all called to "worship Him in spirit and in truth". Worship includes experiencing the presence of God, so that the presence of His Spirit is tangible.

Practicing Freedom

What you do is not nearly as important to God as why you do it.

Identifying why you want to do something – your motive – rather than involvement in the activity itself is at the root of good decision-making. Relationship with God is even greater than the freedom He offers. Love is greatest of all.

The truth is that man longs for rules, but Yeshua encourages relationship instead. That is freeing. Of course there are responsibilities, choices and consequences that come with our actions.

I try to allow every decision to be surrendered to God, remembering "Not my will but yours, Father." (Luke 22:42) and "Perfect love casts out fear." (1John 4:18)

The Culture of Heaven

There is a culture of Heaven that is love, joy, peace... It is not red, olive, black or white. God embraces all culture that is life-giving, and we are each "fearfully and wonderfully made". (Psalm 139:14)

When we give our lives to Yeshua, we become dead to all our old ways of thinking, behaving, and living. Yeshua takes all of our pain – including our anxiety, fear and worry – onto the cross. He gives us a new life so that we don't have to drag the old way of living or thinking around. The old is as dead as a corpse, and if we try to work on changing the old we are only resurrecting a corpse!** Instead, you can discover in your surroundings and circumstances, who you are now, just exactly how God has made you to be.

None of us who follows Yeshua is a citizen of this world any longer

"He who loses his life for my sake will find it" (Matthew 10:39)

As you co-exist in your culture, and walk in the love and freedom you have received from Yeshua, you will discover what the culture of Heaven is, and you will experience the wonderful person God has made you to be.

"Therefore if anyone is in Messiah, he is a new creation. The old things have passed away; behold, all things have become new." (2 Corinthians 5:17 TLV)

You are not a victim or a consequence of your past. Just as Yeshua was crucified on a cross, so you also have been crucified. When Yeshua took on sin, he took on all the thoughts and feelings that are earth-bound and not heavenly. Negative, anxious, bitter, fearful and shameful experiences and feelings no longer are a part of us and we can let them go if we choose. The old is dead and the new is alive and full of hope, joy and peace. The truth is that, through faith, you have received a brand new life with a brand new perspective and brand new possibilities. Nothing has to be as it was before, absolutely nothing. The culture of Heaven meets with the culture of earth through Yeshua, and all of those who believe and follow him.

"Behold, the tabernacle of God *is* with men, and He will dwell with them, and they shall be His people. God Himself will be with them *and be* their God. And God will wipe away every tear from their eyes; there shall be no more death, nor sorrow, nor crying. There shall be no more pain, for the former things have passed away." (Revelation 21:3-4)

* LORD is also a way of addressing the Creator God.

** Some of the New Man perspective is taken from Graham Cooke's teaching in *Arising to a New Identity* and *Game Changers* (https://store.aglow.org/collections/gamechangers/graham-cooke) and my personal discovery and application of it.

AFTERWORD

Testimony of Native American Illustrator Kelly Johnson - when she was a child....

I was playing Basketball with four of my friends Michelle T., Kathy S., MaryAnne, and Dawn N. We were in Michelle's backyard and as we were playing I saw this huge bug on the hedges in the yard. As children you're always curious to new things, and we stopped the game to get an up-close look at it. I did not know what it was then, but it was a very large Green Praying Mantis.

We put him in a jar to get a better look and one by one we held the jar, looking at him. Then my friend Kathy shook the jar and I immediately knew it was wrong to do it, because it was so fragile and was stuck in a jar... Then she handed it to my other friend MaryAnne who followed suit...and my heart got a pain in it. All my mind could think was, 'I saw it, I trapped it, now I am killing it.....' I grabbed the jar and ran home crying, asking God to forgive me for harming His creation.

I ran behind my pool and opened the jar as the Mantis lay there lifeless...and I cried out with all that I was saying..."I am so sorry God, I promise never to harm anything, ever again."

In that moment in time...... I heard His audible voice say to me...

"Do you Promise"?

And I remember being startled thinking, *Who was that...?* And then there was dead silence, and I knew in my own spirit it was God. My Creator and Maker had touched my life with His voice and love. In that moment I needed Him, and in the moment I had asked....

Wow, I stand in Awe today of that amazing encounter that changed my life course.

From that moment on He never left my side. I had free will, but I also was in tune with His will, and following His plan for my life. He kept my crooked path strait, and LIFE overall has been very good for me.

I thank Him with everything that I am, and hope to share how real and alive HE is for all who believe and ask with a whole Heart filled with LOVE, for the ONE who made us.

Smiling... with more to come....

Do you want New Life?

If you want to accept Jesus as your Lord and Saviour, and have not yet, if you believe in the Creator of the universe and want Him as your father, if the Holy Spirit's presence is what you desire in your life, then confess your weaknesses and give them to God.

Ask for and trust in His forgiveness. Confess your faith in Yeshua the son of Creator God, and give your life over to God. Receive the Holy Spirit. Get baptised to seal your new faith. Walk forward, not back and know that you are saved by God's grace and forgiven for all your wayward ways.

When you have committed yourself to God, you can look ahead and walk free. In spiritual terms you are a New Man, free from sin and death. In physical terms, God may choose to heal you immediately or He may want you to overcome step-by-step. But you can trust He is your God and Father and He will never let you go.

Review Request

If you found this book to be helpful and informative, life-giving and hope-inspiring, then I ask you to please pass the message on. One way is by giving it a review on Amazon.

If you know the sort of person who would benefit from it, will you please direct them to it by writing two or three sentences that will inspire them to "look inside".

I'm asking you to please take a minute to leave your rating and comments in the review section of Amazon.

Here is the link to my Author Page to get you there:

http://www.amazon.com/-e/B00J9YXF0

The best time to review is while it's fresh — immediately after reading the book if possible.

Talk about anything you like but here are a few suggestions:

What did you like most about the book?
Is the message different from what you've heard before? How?
Who would you recommend it to?

A review is an amazing way to show your appreciation. And it will help others to discover what you have discovered in these pages.

Thanks in advance!

About the Author

Sarah Tun first visited Constance Lake First Nations Reserve while part of a missionary team which offered a children's summer day camp. She went as part of the annual Bethel Church Kingston team, under Daystar leadership. She loved the people and went back several times, to build friendships and to develop a better understanding of the First Nations. This has enabled her to write this book, which is a unique explanation to the First Nations people, including an invitation to know Yeshua, She offers information and insight beyond a narrow — often prejudiced teaching that was given to previous generations.

Sarah was a secondary school teacher and performing artist before turning to full time writing and ministry. She has a diploma in theology, degrees in drama and education, and life experience from which she draws her counsel. She has been a follower of Jesus for over thirty years. Sarah writes children's fiction, spiritual growth and preaches sermons to encourage all who seek to grow in the knowledge of right and wrong, to discover their call as believers, and to learn what is the goodness of God. A Canadian, she has travelled extensively and enjoyed experiencing life across different cultures. She is married to Alan, and has a step daughter and a son. You can find more of her writings at: http://www.LarusPress.com

www.ingramcontent.com/pod-product-compliance
Lightning Source LLC
Chambersburg PA
CBHW060118050426
42448CB00010B/1921